REPENTANCE AND Revival

JOEL SIEGEL

Repentance and Revival
©2015 Siegel Ministries, Inc.

"I've come to start a fire on this earth—how I wish it were blazing right now! I've come to change everything, turn everything rightside up—how I long for it to be finished!"

Luke 12:49-50 (MSG)

Contents

1
Revival

All at once there was a mighty going, and a mighty rushing wind filled the house. One could feel that the Triune God had moved in much of Heaven's artillery; angels seemed to be standing thick in the church; the Shekinah was there. A stout woman who was sitting in the "Amen corner" jumped to her feet and said, "Sister Jenkins and I do not speak. I want you to pray for me." About that time there was a crash and this woman was stretched out on the floor, knocked down under the power of God. A merchant who was a rival to another merchant (they were not on good terms; there was a coolness) arose in the audience and said, "Mr. Jacobs, if you'll meet me half way, we'll just bury the hatchet, handle and all." They started, but behold! they were knocked down in the aisle; they did not get to each other. A schoolteacher got up to say something but fell sprawling. There were thirteen prostrations and thirty-three running up and down the aisle shouting, and sixteen or seventeen swept into the kingdom. On Sunday night in this revival, twenty rushed to the altar at the first call, twenty came at the second call, and all forty were gloriously saved. (Praying Clear Through, Rev. William Harney, 74-75)

This account from the turn of the twentieth century stirs something in me. I love the genuineness, the spontaneity, the raw power. This story is an example of *revival*: a move of God that cannot be scripted, controlled, or manufactured, only prepared for, received, and cooperated with.

Revival is similar to what many people call *a move of God*, or *an outpouring*. A move of God blossoms into revival as it gains momentum, spreading into the hearts and lives of God's people. Lives are changed and, indeed, people who may have been saved for years find their whole world turned upside down (or right-side up, to be more accurate). A true revival will spread like fire – extending out into the world – with many lost souls coming to the saving knowledge of Christ.

It's foretold in Scripture, and has been prophesied by many of God's servants, that the return of Christ will be preceded by a great worldwide revival. (I speak of this last-days revival extensively in my book *The Coming Of The Lord*.) We are actually in this revival now, albeit in the beginning stages. The revival that will lead us into Christ's return must grow and spread in intensity until God's power has flooded the earth, causing a great harvest of souls to be reaped. The last-days revival will indeed be a great move of God.

A MOVE OF GOD

It seems as though I rarely preach without using the phrase *a move of God*, but that phrase is somewhat of a misnomer. There's really no such thing as a move of God in the sense of God moving all by Himself. When we speak of God's movement, the movement of His body is always included. God's movement is always to be a collaboration between the Head (Christ) and His Body (the Church). Indeed, there is little that God does in the earth all by Himself. If He desires to move in a service, and His Body refuses to move with Him, the result is the same as if He never moved in the first place. Nothing happens.

A *move of God*, therefore, is the movement of God and His people together. This takes place through a series of *initiations* and *responses*. Often, God will initiate movement through the promptings of His Spirit. At other times, He allows us to initiate movement and He graciously responds (as we join our hearts in worship, for example). There must be both an initiation and an appropriate response in order for God to move.

We can look back in Church history and recount great moves of God: times of prolonged, effective revival. America in particular has been the blessed recipient of the outpouring of God's power. Even secular historians mark periods in American history known as the *First Great Awakening* (1700's) and the *Second Great Awakening* (1800's).

During the Second Great Awakening, it's documented that, under the preaching of Rev. Charles G. Finney, bars and theaters in Rochester, New York closed due to lack of patronage. In one year's time, the churches in town swelled with over one hundred thousand new converts. Friends, that's revival. That's a move of God. That's an outpouring. But none of it was God moving all by Himself. It took the cooperation of His body in an ongoing series of initiations and responses.

Many of us have solicited God in prayer for His outpouring – for a great revival – and we are right to do so. However, we would be incorrect to think that once we have prayed, everything is left in the Father's hands. Nothing could be further from the truth. It's true that prayer is of great importance, and God certainly must do the part that only He can do. However, we must not deceive ourselves, thinking that once we have prayed, our job is done. No, we have an ongoing part to play in the move of God. We must make movement along with Him, responding not just occasionally, but continually.

I recently heard a well-respected minister state that although every revival is a move of God, not every move of God is a revival. In other words, there are components other than the outpouring of God that must be present to constitute real revival. Just having God's power flow in the room is not enough; something must also happen *in* God's people.

God can be moving among His Church, and His Church be cooperating in only a limited fashion. This is too often the case. A congregation may go along with the move of God to a degree, but stop short of continuing on with Him into the fulness that He desires. They get thrilled with how God moved in a particular service, but then go about their lives as though nothing happened. When people are so quickly satisfied, that's not revival. Revival takes place when the hearts of the people unite with the purposes of God, and all thoughts of self and schedule dissipate.

It's time for revival and it's not God that's holding it back. We can have it anytime we want it.

2
Hunger

God, I've heard what our ancestors say about you,
and I'm stopped in my tracks, down on my knees. **Do**
among us what you did among them. Work among
us as you worked among them. *And as you bring*
judgment, as you surely must, remember mercy.
Habakkuk 3:2 (MSG)

Although I wasn't around for the Great Awakenings of centuries past, I'm certain I have experienced revival, at least to a degree. I know what they look like. I've seen the lines of people wrap around church buildings as they wait for hours to get in. I've seen people fly in from around the world just to be at the meetings in person. I've been there when thousands of people were *out under the power* at once, their bodies night after night filling the floor, stage, and even the hallways. There's a distinctness about revival: a level of spiritual energy that's different from what we might call *church as usual.*

TWO SCHOOLS

I was born again just before starting college at the University of Miami, in Coral Gables, Florida, and it wasn't long before I was on-fire for God. I became so engrossed with the things of God that my schooling probably suffered as a result. I was sharing Christ with anyone who would listen and many people were being saved. I started teaching people the Word of God and, along with a few good friends, started a weekly Bible study on campus.

My friends and I took turns teaching that Bible study. We knew just enough to be dangerous, but that Bible study grew until we had difficulty finding places to meet. It made such an impact on the campus that, ten years after I graduated, I heard that our weekly study was still in existence. (I pray that it continues to this day.) Some of the people that were saved during that time are in full-time ministry today. It was a move of God.

As great as that time was for myself and others, I cannot say that it was true revival. I wouldn't have known it at the time, but, looking back, I can see some missing elements. What we had was more like youthful enthusiasm than revival. (There's nothing wrong with enthusiasm; it's better than indifference.) That study group was great, but it was not revival.

I graduated from college and moved to Rochester, New York (home of the great Finney revivals) to attend graduate school at the Eastman School of Music. It was there that, for the first time, I experienced revival. It was right there on campus: an entire group of believers who were fully radicalized, like me. I was so glad to have found them.

What was the difference between the group in Miami and the group in Rochester? If I could sum it up in one word, it would be *hunger*. There was a hunger among the Christians in my school in Rochester that just wasn't quite there in Miami.

Was the doctrine any better in Rochester? No, it actually may have been worse. No one really cared about doctrine though, they were just hungry for God. (Doctrine is important, of course. God promises to confirm *His Word* with signs following, not beliefs that we make up.)

These people had to have more of God, see more of God, and share more of God. The mission? Get everyone in the school saved. There were prayer groups and Bible studies happening somewhere in the building every single day. We would find out who was open to the gospel and pray them in. Resistance was futile. There was no time for TV, movies, sports, or social events; we were doing the work of God.

About ten percent of the student body was serving God and meeting together weekly for worship (besides going to their respective churches on Sundays). Something happened every single day. Someone got saved or filled with the Spirit. Someone was either getting a demon cast out of them or receiving one (as I said, it wasn't all scriptural). There was such hunger that we didn't know if we were trying to keep up with God, or if He was trying to keep up with us.

Why was there more hunger there than on my college campus in Miami? I'm not sure I know all the reasons, but I am sure I know one. The people at Eastman paid a greater price to commit to Jesus.

PAYING THE PRICE

This was a small school of several hundred people, not the sprawling diverse campus with thousands of students that I had come from. If you got saved at Eastman, everyone knew it. Not everyone celebrated it, however. This school was highly competitive, highly intellectual, and high-stress. Just to be there was a privilege that only a few enjoyed. There was no room for non-conformity and there was no room for God. The people that received Christ knew it was going to cost them. They would be talked about and perhaps ostracized. They didn't care. They were too hungry, and the little bit of persecution that they may have endured was just enough to keep a fire lit under everybody. You were in or out. No middle ground. No lukewarm. No cheap Christianity.

I'll never forget one girl who was saved at Eastman. She was having great difficulty adjusting to the rigors of conservatory life and was quite a basket case. Thankfully, she got born again and changed instantly. The glow on her face made it apparent that something radical had happened to her. Her parents, worried about her fragile state, had been keeping close tabs on her. When they found out that she had been saved, they did not rejoice. Instead, they pulled her out of school and checked her into a mental hospital. That's called paying a price for what you believe! The moment she got saved and stable, her parents flipped out and had her committed. Thanks, Mom and Dad.

People who have grown up in the things of God don't always appreciate the greatness of the gift that they have in Christ and can be prone to complacency. No, they are not at a disadvantage, for the greatest advantage one can have is a life that has never been lived for the devil. But they must be careful not to take the Lord for granted. Perhaps they haven't paid the price initially that others have had to pay, but as they grow in godliness, they will pay. Everyone who moves into a deeper relationship with God will experience opposition.

> *Indeed, all who desire to live a godly life in Christ Jesus will be persecuted.*
>
> 2 Timothy 3:12

Stay Hungry

> *Spiritually prosperous are those hungering and thirsting for righteousness, because they themselves shall be filled so as to be completely satisfied.*
>
> Matthew 5:6 (WST)

In the 2012 superhero movie *The Avengers*, the team of freedom fighters was a far cry from what one would call perfect chemistry. By far, though, the biggest problem was the hero known as *The Hulk*. He couldn't control his power and would destroy everything in sight. In order to become the Hulk, Dr.

Bruce Banner would have to be provoked to rage. He left the group for a season, later returning with greater control over his power, able to turn into the Hulk at will. Dr. Banner told the other avengers the secret of his newfound control: *I stay angry*, was his explanation.

Just as Dr. Banner learned to stay angry in order to become something greater than his human self, we must learn to stay hungry, so we too can become greater. Staying hungry is the Christian's occupation. It's wrong for a believer to lose their hunger and possess a take-it-or-leave-it attitude. Never allow yourself to become complacent, ceasing to follow after God. Stay hot for God. Stay hungry.

> *The secret of spiritual success is a hunger that persists.*
>
> *(Smith Wigglesworth)*

SATISFIED

Is it right or wrong to be satisfied? Both. The Christian must see satisfaction as a very temporary state, similar to the way we are satisfied after a meal. When someone serves me something wonderful, I will eat until I am satisfied. My satisfaction at meal time is not a permanent condition, however. In just a few more hours I'll be hungry again, and, if there are leftovers from the great meal that I just had, my hunger climbs to an even higher level, becoming a craving. A craving for something that's sitting just a few rooms away is different than when there's nothing in the refrigerator. It's a greater hunger, one that justifies an extra snack or an earlier meal.

This is how we must be with the things of God. When the service is done and the anointing lifts, we can be satisfied *for now*, but not satisfied *for good*. The experience we just had makes us hungry for more, because we know there's plenty more available. As our experience with God grows, our hunger grows. It takes more to satisfy us now than it did in the past.

> *I am satisfied with the dissatisfaction that never rests until it is satisfied and satisfied again.*
>
> *(Smith Wigglesworth)*

Addicted

Some years ago, I heard a pop/jazz song by a secular music group that I had grown up listening to. The main lyric of that song was *Once you get a taste, there's no turning back.*

I immediately thought of the scripture in Psalm 34:8 which says, *Oh, taste and see that the Lord is good!* I had great hopes that this song was based on the Word of God. As I listened closely, however, I discovered that the song was actually talking about people with drug habits, not people pursuing the things of God. I was disappointed, but the song's message was true nonetheless: once you get a taste, there's no turning back.

There are some drugs that are so addictive that, if you use them even once, you're hooked. You can't turn back. Nor are you satisfied with the same dose that got you started. The drug user needs more and more of their preferred substance in order to be satisfied. Nothing can take the place of their daily fix.

The Christian ought to be at least as hungry for the things of God as the drug addict is for their drug. I have known drug addicts who have committed unspeakable acts just to get one more dose of their drug. They would do things that they would never normally do, just to achieve temporary satisfaction.

I have tasted of the things of God. It started with just a few scriptures, but I got hooked. I had to hear them again and read them again. Before I knew it, those few verses turned into a few chapters. Then I found out about church, where everyone would come and hear the Word together. I developed a three-times-a-week church habit. That turned into witnessing, prayer, and the ministry of helps. Before I knew it, I was practically in ministry. It all started with that first taste.

A few years later, I was filled with the Spirit, speaking in other tongues. That's the Christian's heroin. Soon after, I went to a service where I saw the anointing in manifestation. Just one taste and I was hooked. For years now, I've been an anointing junkie. The little taste I started out with doesn't satisfy me like it used to. I need large, frequent doses of God's power. There's no cure for me; I've gone too far and can't turn back. I don't want to turn back. I want more, and I'll do whatever it takes to get it. I've accepted the fact that my God-addiction is a life-long condition.

Where are the Christians who are hopeless God-addicts? The ones who will sell anything and move anywhere, doing whatever it takes to follow after God? Where are the ones who have that look in their eyes that says, *I've got to have more. I know there's another level?*

Where are the ones who leave satisfied on Sunday morning, only to need another fix by Sunday afternoon? God's looking for those who hunger and thirst after Him: those who *have* to have more of Him and will not be denied.

> *God—you're my God! I can't get enough of you! I've worked up such hunger and thirst for God, traveling across dry and weary deserts. So here I am in the place of worship, eyes open, drinking in your strength and glory.*
>
> *Psalms 63:1-2 (MSG)*

3
Passion

We have identified hunger as a prominent characteristic of revival. Closely associated with hunger is passion. Passion is a relentless desire. It's a love that pursues. It must always be found in the believer, never being allowed to wane.

> Go and shout this message to Jerusalem. This is what the Lord says: "I remember how eager you were to please me as a young bride long ago, how you loved me and followed me even through the barren wilderness."
>
> Jeremiah 2:2 (NLT)

In this verse, we see God reaching out to Israel, disappointed with the present state of their relationship. He was saying, in essence, *Things aren't they way they used to be. You've changed.*

Most of us have seen the movie or TV show where the husband and wife are sitting up on opposite edges of the bed, each engrossed with their own books or hobbies. The wife may turn to the husband and say with exasperation, *Look at us. What's happened to us?* She's disappointed that the relationship has turned into something other than the constant flow of love and passion that they had when they started.

Our Lord should never have to come to us and say, *What's happened to us?* It's not normal for an intimate relationship to grow stale. When that happens, it means that one or both parties in the relationship have drifted away, allowing things to fall into decline. Where our relationship with the Lord is concerned, He never drifts. It could only be us.

The Lord expressed frustration with the fact that, as long as they were in barren places of difficulty, the people stuck to Him like glue. This passage in Jeremiah 2 goes on to show, however, that as soon as the pressure eased and the situation turned around, they moved on. God forbid that should ever be the case with us.

In Love with Him

> *But I have this against you, that you have abandoned the love you had at first. Remember therefore from where you have fallen; repent, and do the works you did at first. If not, I will come to you and remove your lampstand from its place, unless you repent.*
>
> *Revelation 2:4-5*

Jesus spoke these strong words to the church at Ephesus. The church at Ephesus was one of the best churches of the day. As one reads Paul's letter to this church, it's evident that they walked in a degree of spiritual maturity that some other churches did not. Even so, Jesus put His finger on a major issue. With all they were doing for God, they had let themselves grow out of one very important aspect of their relationship: they fell out of love with Him. You can't do that and expect revival.

As Christians grow and develop, start families, buy houses, get better jobs, etc. they must be careful not to grow out of the love affair they once had with the Father. They must not cease to be excited at the possibility of reaching just one new soul. Frequently take inventory of your relationship with God. Never let your love run cold or become choked out by other projects. Stay in love with Jesus.

> *I know your works: you are neither cold nor hot. Would that you were either cold or hot! So, because you are lukewarm, and neither hot nor cold, I will spit you out of my mouth. For you say, I am rich, I have prospered, and I need nothing, not realizing that you are wretched, pitiable, poor, blind, and naked. I counsel you to buy from me gold refined by fire, so that you may be rich, and white garments so that you may clothe yourself and the shame of your nakedness may not be seen, and salve to anoint your eyes, so that you may see. Those whom I love, I reprove and discipline, so be zealous and repent.*
> *Revelation 3:15-19*

This is yet another passage showing the Lord's attitude toward those who fail to maintain their spiritual love life. Notice the strong language of verse 16 in the Message translation:

You're stale. You're stagnant. You make me want to vomit.

I don't think the Lord could be more clear or say it any stronger. It's simply not okay for us to take our foot off the gas of our relationship with Christ and just coast along. It's not right to be less *on-fire* today than at any other point in our life. Our love for Him and knowledge of Him should grow with each new day.

It's absolutely disgusting to the Lord for Him to see any one of us sink down into the lethargy of life in the flesh when He's provided a high-octane, supercharged quality of life for us. It's nauseating to Him to see us act disinterested and become disengaged with His things when He's given us all things pertaining to life and godliness. It's a major slap in His face for us to turn back or turn aside when He wants to shine His light and burn His holy fire through us. We must live completely sold-out to Christ. All the time. Anything less is unacceptable.

If we say we want revival, then we want the hot, passionate, living relationship that Jesus has always required of His followers. Total commitment. Total surrender. Complete abandonment of the natural. Our hand to the plow, with no looking back.

I spoke in the previous chapter of the two colleges I attended. Many people at each place loved God, but the people at the one school pressed in more, were hungrier, and had a passion for God that just wouldn't quit. We would sit in a circle for extended periods of time just waiting quietly and worshipping in His presence. We would drive hours for the opportunity to share our faith at a local church, for free. We would do anything for God. We *had* to do something for God, and it had to be now. You couldn't tell us no. You couldn't shut us up. That's why we had revival. It didn't just fall upon us. It was in us. We carried it everywhere we went.

What must we do if revival seems to have eluded us? What if we see that our life has fallen short of the standards described in the passages we have looked at? Well, we don't give up, and we don't heap condemnation upon ourselves. The answers are simple, contained in the passages we have already read:

> *Remember therefore from where you have fallen; **repent**, and do the works you did at first. If not, I will come to you and remove your lampstand from its place, **unless you repent**.*
>
> *Revelation 2:5*

> *Those whom I love, I reprove and discipline, so **be zealous and repent**.*
>
> *Revelation 3:19*

What will move us from where we are to full-fledged revival? Repentance. Certainly, there are also other components such as faith and prayer, however, repentance is one of the things we are missing right now in the Body of Christ. We will spend the next several chapters speaking about it.

Before assuming that you know what repentance is all about, consider the following:

In 1987, a movie called *The Princess Bride* was released, becoming an instant classic. The film starts out following the crooked *Vizzini* and his two not-so-crooked hired hands, *Inigo Montoya* and *Fezzik*, as they try to capture a princess and hold her for ransom.

Every time a situation goes differently than Vizzini anticipated (which is all the time), he exclaims, *Inconceivable!* He uses this word at least a half-dozen times in the course of just a few minutes. Finally, the soft-spoken Inigo Montoya looks at him and, with heavily-accented English, utters this now-famous reply:

> *You keep using that word. I do not think it means what you think it means.*

Christians everywhere are familiar with the word *repentance* and most have an idea of what it means to repent. We need, however, to explore the Scriptures for a closer look. Repentance is a broader subject than many have realized. Although people keep using that word, *it does not mean what they think it means.*

4

Foundations

---

*Therefore let us leave the elementary doctrine of Christ
and go on to maturity, not laying again a foundation
of repentance from dead works and of faith toward
God, and of instruction about washings, the laying
on of hands, the resurrection of the dead,
and eternal judgment.*
Hebrews 6:1-2

The writer of Hebrews was expressing displeasure with the lack of spiritual progress in the lives of the believers to whom he was writing. They were not able to receive truth on a deeper level, and were being poor stewards of truths they had already received. Notice this statement, just a few verses earlier:

*For though by this time you ought to be teachers, you
need someone to teach you again the basic principles of
the oracles of God. You need milk, not solid food.*
Hebrews 5:12

The phrases *basic principles, elementary doctrine,* and *laying again a foundation* are used in this passage. Basic, elementary, foundational. The writer is talking about the ABC's of our faith here: truths with which every believer should be familiar. The

Hebrew Christians needed to be taught these truths all over again; they had treated these things casually and had let them slip.

This list of basic truths is quite interesting. One of them is *faith toward God*. Every believer must be established in the principles of faith before they can go on to maturity. The subject of faith, much maligned in our day, is not something for so-called *advanced believers*, nor is it something for just a few specially-gifted believers. Faith – believing and receiving from God – is for everybody. It's how a person receives Christ, and it's to be part of the foundation upon which we build our spiritual life.

Listed next is *instructions about washings*. The Greek word translated as *washings* is the word *baptismos*, often translated as *baptisms*. The believer should understand the different baptisms mentioned in the New Testament. First, at salvation, the believer is baptized, or placed, into the Body of Christ. (That's the *one baptism* mentioned in Ephesians 4:5.) Second, believers should follow the Lord's command to participate in water baptism: an outward testimony of an inward change. Third, every believer should receive the Baptism of the Holy Spirit with the evidence of speaking in other tongues. These are the three major baptisms spoken of in the Word. Believers should not be confused about this topic (as many are), but should instead be established in the truth.

The laying on of hands is mentioned next. How interesting that this practice, not even permitted in many churches, is to be elementary to the believer. The different purposes for the laying on of hands include *transmission, impartation,* and *blessing.* The laying on of hands is used to minister healing (transmitting God's healing power), to separate people to a ministry calling (imparting spiritual gifts), to receive the Baptism of the Holy Spirit, and to simply bless people, including children. Thank God for this foundational doctrine.

The resurrection of the dead and eternal judgement. Believers must understand that life doesn't end when we die here on earth. That's true for the unbeliever as well as for us. All will rise again and receive eternal judgement. Eternal means *forever.* Are we settled and established in the fact that the unbeliever will die in his sins and spend eternity in hell, or are we only established in the truths regarding heaven? If we say that we are established, surely we will help others miss the torments of an eternity without God.

The believer too has an eternal destiny and will face judgement for the things he or she has done (or failed to do) here on earth. There is much to be taught along these lines.

Of course, we purposely skipped the first topic listed in our text: *repentance from dead works.* How significant that this subject tops the list. Is this just speaking about leaving our old life behind and turning to God? No. It would include that, but that's not all the phrase means.

Many would say that all of these elementary truths are just speaking about the salvation experience: repent from sin, have faith in Christ, be baptized in water and make heaven your eternal home. It's true, salvation is where it all starts for the believer, but if that's *all* this was talking about, the writer of Hebrews wouldn't be telling them that they needed to hear it again. (After all, we're only born again, water baptized, etc. one time.) No, they were being prodded to go into crisis-mode to re-establish themselves, because there are ongoing, critical aspects to each of these truths, including repentance.

Far from a one-time event, repentance is an ongoing part of the believer's life. It's as much a part of our life as faith or the fullness of the Spirit. It is an area not to be ignored.

5
Empty Energy

---

*Therefore let us leave the elementary doctrine of Christ
and go on to maturity, not laying again a foundation of
repentance from dead works and of faith toward God.*
Hebrews 6:1

If repentance is to be an ongoing part of our life, then the things
from which we are to repent must also be ongoing. Here, we
are told to repent from *dead works*.

All Christians would probably agree that *dead works* sounds
like a picture of our life before Christ. I would not dispute that,
as there's a sense in which one's entire life before Christ could
be considered a *dead work*. However, this phrase is not just a
look-back at our lost condition. Repentance from dead works
wouldn't be included as a foundational part of our life if it only
pertained to our unsaved past. There must be a sense in which it
applies to the believer's present life.

LEAVE AND GO ON

Let's back up just a bit further to make sure we understand
this passage correctly. The Hebrew believers were encouraged
to *leave the elementary doctrine of Christ and go on to maturity,*

not laying again a foundation. . . . Notice that they were told to *leave* and *go on*. Let's clarify what is meant by the word *leave*. It's obvious that the writer wasn't telling the believers to leave these things *behind*, rather he was telling them to leave these things *in place*. How can we be sure? Because he was speaking about a foundation that had been laid. Foundations are not temporary structures that get disposed of when it's time to build higher. The foundation is the most essential, permanent part of a building, never to be moved. You lay the foundation, and then leave it right where it is and go on, building higher and higher.

These foundational doctrines are an ongoing part of the believer's life, just like the alphabet is an ongoing part of every person's life. I don't recite the alphabet or sing the alphabet song anymore, however, the alphabet is a permanent part of me: the foundation of my language. I never forget my ABC's and leave them behind. On the contrary, I need those letters now more than ever.

These foundational areas of our faith shouldn't be foreign to the believer but should be second nature. One of these truths is *repentance from dead works*. How much preaching have you heard along these lines? Because this subject might be new to some people, we must take time to understand exactly what it means. First we'll define *dead works*, and then we'll define *repentance*.

Dead Works

Can a born again believer (one who is alive to God) really have something in their life that's dead? Sure. When something is dead, it's void of life. We could say it's *empty*. (When the Bible speaks of death, it never means that the person or thing ceases to exist. Death, in the Bible, means *separation from life*.)

The word *works* is the Greek word *ergon*, from which we get our English word *ergonomics*. *Ergon* means *effort, toil,* or *energy*. When something is a *dead work*, we could say it's *empty energy*. The effort, or energy, was expended, but it was empty, accomplishing nothing.

What would make someone's efforts empty? For the believer, an activity is empty if God's not in it. God is the one who breathes life into our efforts, making them fruitful. If He's not in what we're doing, our efforts are in vain: they are *empty energy*. The Bible also uses the phrase *in the flesh* to speak of things that are done without God. It's possible to do something *for* God, but without God. This is something every Christian needs to be aware of. It's easy to think that if what you're doing is a good thing, it's automatically a God-thing. Not so.

What does it mean for God to be *in* something? It means the activity is either based on the written Word of God, done in response to the leading of the Spirit, or, best of all, both. It means that what we're doing is God's plan, not just our own plan. When God's in it, there's power behind it. When man just decides on His own to do something, it's empty, even if well-intentioned.

We must stop calling things *the work of God* just because natural energy is being expended. It's possible that the energy that we're using is empty.

I could take my car and jack it up so that the wheels are no longer touching the ground. I could then get inside, start the car, put it in gear, and begin to act as though I'm driving. The engine is running, the wheels are spinning, I am turning the wheel, but I'm not going anywhere. Is energy being expended? Yes, but it's empty energy: a lot of noise, but I'm just going through the motions. Giving the car more gas won't do anything but burn more fuel, because there's a missing link: the car is not on the ground where progress can be made.

Paul spoke of these kinds of empty activities: things that appear productive on the outside, but are really nothing more than a lot of noise.

If I speak in the tongues of men and of angels, but have not love, I am a noisy gong or a clanging cymbal.

1 Corinthians 13:1

It's possible to be working for God, but those works still be considered dead works (i.e., God didn't author it, He's not in it). It's even possible to have a dead service, or go to a dead church. There are a variety of activities that look and sound spiritual but are nothing more than empty energy. Let's resolve that the things that we do will be His plan, done His way. We like to think we can make up our own plans and then pray, asking Him to come alongside and bless it, but that's deception. Let your efforts be God-birthed and God-directed. Does this all sound strange? It shouldn't. Here's one of the many scriptures that should steer us away from empty energy:

> *Anyone who builds on that foundation may use a variety of materials—gold, silver, jewels, wood, hay, or straw. But on the judgment day, fire will reveal what kind of work each builder has done. The fire will show if a person's work has any value. If the work survives, that builder will receive a reward. But if the work is burned up, the builder will suffer great loss. The builder will be saved, but like someone barely escaping through a wall of flames.*
>
> *1 Corinthians 3:12-15 (NLT)*

Not all work is productive for the kingdom. Not all busy-ness is progress. Because we all have flesh, we know it's possible to be operating *in the flesh*. We want to instead operate from our living relationship with Christ, receiving direction from Him and flowing with His plan. The believer is responsible to monitor and identify whether his or her works are dead, or God-filled. If God's in it, great. Keep going, but stay aware. It's possible to start out in the spirit but transition over into the flesh (see Galatians 3:3). If we see that God is not in our efforts, what must we do? Repent.

Please don't misunderstand me. I'm not saying that it's wrong to work a secular job or to run a secular business. It's actually wrong *not* to work. My point is, God should be in it. Is the job you are working something that supports your family? Fine. That's scriptural. Even better, do you sense that the things you are doing are part of His divine plan for your life? Great! There are, unfortunately, many believers who step out into activities (even ministries) into which God did not direct them. That's empty energy.

I know this may be different than what first comes to mind when hearing the phrase *dead works*, however, there's nothing in this phrase or passage to suggest that it's only speaking of our lost condition, or just referring to what we would call gross sinful behavior. We are quick to think of stealing money, lying to one's spouse, watching an unwholesome movie, etc. as *dead works*. If those things are occurring in your life, they are indeed dead, but those things should never be occurring in the believer's life. Again, the phrase *empty energy* gives us a more accurate picture of what the Bible is really saying. If God's not in what we're doing, it's empty. We must repent.

First Works

*Remember therefore from whence thou art fallen, and repent, and **do the first works**; or else I will come unto thee quickly, and will remove thy candlestick out of his place, except thou repent. Revelation 2:5 (KJV)*

Do you know what Jesus meant when He told the Church to *do the first works?* The Greek word translated as *first* is the same word translated as *forward*. Do you remember the Greek word for *works?* It's *ergon,* meaning *energy. First works,* therefore, means *forward energy.* I like that! Just as it's possible to expend empty energy, it's also possible to move ahead with forward energy: not just spinning your wheels but having your faith in gear.

What does this have to do with revival? A lot. Revival is the opposite of that which is dead or empty. If we want revival, that means we want God inhabiting our efforts, adding His supernatural power to our natural movement. He stands ready to fill our every activity, but only when those activities are part of His flow. When we depart from His flow, our energy is empty. When we flow with Him, we move forward. We are to recognize what kind of energy is moving in our life, and, if we find that it's empty, repent.

6

Repentance

Therefore I despise myself, and
repent in dust and ashes.
Job 42:6

Repentance isn't a bad word, it's a Bible word: a life-giving truth. When people hear about repentance, they often think of scriptures like the one above. They picture someone sitting around depressed, with sackcloth on their back and ashes on their head, hating their very existence. (No wonder most people would rather not hear about repentance, much less ever have to do it.) What they may not understand, however, is the power that repentance brings. It was repentance that caused Job's hopeless situation to dramatically turn for the better. In fact, Job, after he repented, was by far the most blessed man on earth. It's a good thing to repent.

Repentance has been the victim of a narrow view and has been given a bad rap, largely because its meaning has been misunderstood. Although sorrow can sometimes be involved, sorrow and repentance are not the same thing. The dust-and-ashes picture alone should not shape our concept of repentance, for that is actually the least frequent way that it occurs. It is a multi-faceted word with a broad application for the believer. Consider the following example:

THE EXAMPLE OF PRAYER

My spiritual father, Rev. Kenneth E. Hagin, taught extensively on the subject of prayer. Prayer is something that every believer should practice but, because the Bible gives many different examples of prayer, it's easy to end up confused as to how best to pray. As Brother Hagin studied this subject carefully, he discovered that prayer can take on different forms, each one being practiced somewhat differently.

For example, two of the most common forms of prayer are the prayer of faith (where the believer receives something that God has promised) and the prayer of consecration (dedication to God's will and plan). The difference between these two types of prayer is that the first is based on the revealed will of God while the second centers around the unknown will of God. These two kinds of prayer couldn't be more different, yet they both qualify as prayer: communicating with God.

During the prayer of consecration, one might include the phrase *if it be your will* as they dedicate themselves to God's plan. That same phrase would be inappropriate, however, if used in the prayer of faith, where His will is already known. The believer who wants to be effective in prayer must distinguish between prayer's forms. To ignore the different kinds of prayer is as erroneous as ignoring different kinds of sports, choosing instead to play every game using only the rules of baseball. You can hit home runs in tennis if you want, but that's not the point of the game. Not all sports are the same; not all prayer is the same.

These illustrations apply to the subject of repentance, as well. There are many forms of repentance, with only the most dramatic being widely recognized. The sackcloth and ashes scenario is but one form of this great truth.

UNDERSTANDING REPENTANCE

The Greek word translated as *repentance* is *metanoia*, meaning *a change of mind*. It means *to think differently*. The thought of a change in action or direction would also be included. Sorrow and tears may or may not be involved, and, although repentance is most often seen in Scripture in connection with sin, this is not always the case. As we have already seen, the term is not just applied to sinners coming to Christ for the first time, but also to believers (Hebrews 6:1). Additionally, there are times when even God is said to have repented.

Notice this passage, in which the city of Nineveh responded to the preaching of the Prophet Jonah:

> *So Jonah arose, and went unto Nineveh, according to the word of the Lord. Now Nineveh was an exceeding great city of three days' journey. And Jonah began to enter into the city a day's journey, and he cried, and said, Yet forty days, and Nineveh shall be overthrown. So the people of Nineveh believed God, and proclaimed a fast, and put*

on sackcloth, from the greatest of them even to the least of them. For word came unto the king of Nineveh, and he arose from his throne, and he laid his robe from him, and covered him with sackcloth, and sat in ashes. And he caused it to be proclaimed and published through Nineveh by the decree of the king and his nobles, saying, Let neither man nor beast, herd nor flock, taste any thing: let them not feed, nor drink water: But let man and beast be covered with sackcloth, and cry mightily unto God: yea, let them turn every one from his evil way, and from the violence that is in their hands. Who can tell if God will turn and repent, and turn away from his fierce anger, that we perish not? And God saw their works, that they turned from their evil way; and God repented of the evil, that he had said that he would do unto them; and he did it not.

Jonah 3:3-10 (KJV)

Everybody repented in this passage. First, Jonah repented for his disobedience, finally following God's command to preach to Nineveh. Then, the king repented for having allowed his city to fall into judgement. Next, the people of Nineveh followed their king's lead, repenting for their sinful behavior. Finally, God repented of His plan to destroy the city.

God, of course, had done nothing wrong, but He did change His mind. That's what repentance is all about: change. Because there was repentance across-the-board (in Jonah, the king, the people of Nineveh, and God), a kingdom avoided destruction and was set on the right course. Repentance, in this case, saved a city from destruction. Repentance saves lives.

It doesn't seem so bad now, does it?

It Starts in the Heart

Repentance is *a change of mind*, but we understand that spiritual things never start in the mind, they start in the heart: in the spirit of man. Heart-change is what real repentance is all about. When change occurs in the attitude of one's heart, the mind takes its cue and begins to think accordingly.

A person can have right actions but a wrong heart. We see this often as we endeavor to correct our children. We may tell them to go take care of something that they should have done earlier. They roll their eyes, gasp, grumble, stomp, slam doors, and do a half-hearted job so they can get back to texting their friends. As parents, we must recognize that as long as this continues, our correction toward them is not finished. That child still needs to repent. They need a change of heart: a renewed attitude that teaches their mind not to act like a fool when interacting with the people that gave birth to them.

When training others in life, ministry, work, etc. we want their heart, not just their actions. God is the same way. He sees the heart; He's all about the heart. He'll keep training us and correcting us until He sees the necessary change in our heart and in our actions.

We can begin to see the place that repentance has in the life of the believer. The Christian life is a progression – one change after another – as the believer conforms to the image of Christ. Of course, repentance is also to be found in the heart of the sinner who desires to come to Christ. It's the first spiritual act in which a lost person engages.

A Misunderstood Subject

Repentance is greatly misunderstood among believers. Many consider it an outdated, old-fashioned, unnecessary concept, not fit for the presentation of the good news that we preach today. Those who market their church as *the fun church in town* might have a difficult time preaching repentance. Many churches and preachers have scrubbed it from their presentation of the gospel, but it must be included in the gospel.

We've heard many preach, *Just come as you are and receive.*

No. Come as you are, repent, and receive.

Receiving follows repenting. You cannot have one without the other. These two words are connected.

Repenting and Receiving

When the sinner comes to Christ, he or she must repent. What does that mean? A change of heart and mind about their entire life. The person must agree that their own works have failed to produce righteousness and that sin has prevailed. (You cannot be saved if you don't understand that you need a Savior.) Then they must agree that Jesus took care of their sin, choosing to submit to His lordship. The repentant sinner is one who is ready for change. Major change. Big change. If you don't want change, you don't want Jesus.

We don't require people to change their lives before receiving Christ, because the kind of change they need is the kind that only God can produce. It would be unfair to require people to do what only God can do. No person can change the condition of his or her heart. They can, however, change the *position* (or attitude) of their heart. They can have an open, submissive heart, rather than one that is stubborn and hard. This is repentance, and it's required. If a person won't repent, they won't be saved.

> *Therefore let the whole house of Israel recognize beyond all doubt and acknowledge assuredly that God has made Him both Lord and Christ (the Messiah)—this Jesus Whom you crucified. Now when they heard this **they were stung (cut) to the heart**, and they said to Peter and the rest of the apostles (special messengers), Brethren, what shall we do? And Peter answered them, **Repent (change your views and purpose to accept the will of God in your inner selves instead of rejecting it)** and be baptized, every one of you, in the name of Jesus Christ for the forgiveness of and release from your sins; and you shall receive the gift of the Holy Spirit.*
>
> *Acts 2:36-38 (AMP)*

How precious this is. They heard the gospel and it penetrated their hearts. They didn't get offended and walk out, rather, they recognized that this was God at work. They also recognized that they didn't presently qualify for God's gift of eternal life, so they asked Peter, *What shall we do?* The answer he gave them is the same answer for today: *Repent and receive.* Be ready for change. When a person is open to change, they can receive. When their hearts are hard and unyielding, they cannot receive. What did these people do? They repented and received.

> *So those who received his word were baptized, and there were added that day about three thousand souls.*
>
> *Acts 2:41*

Here's another verse that shows that the sinner must repent in order to receive Christ:

> *The times of ignorance God overlooked, but now he commands all people everywhere to repent.*
>
> *Acts 17:30*

It's interesting that God didn't command them to pray, He didn't tell them to reform, He didn't tell them to attend services. The command was to repentance: they were to position their hearts for change.

> *Therefore, O King Agrippa, I was not disobedient to the heavenly vision, but declared first to those in Damascus, then in Jerusalem and throughout all the region of Judea, and also to the Gentiles, that they should **repent and turn to God**, performing deeds in keeping with their repentance.*
>
> *Acts 26:19-20*

Again, repentance is not left out of the message of salvation, as is so often the case in our day of *soft Christianity*. They were to *repent and turn*: a change of position and a change of direction. When we share the gospel with the lost, we must let them know to get ready for big change. If they are not willing to hear that, do not allow them to pray the sinner's prayer. They cannot receive until they repent.

Are we restricting the gospel? Is this bad news? No, it's amazing news. The change that God brings to the sinner will revolutionize his or her life. It will be beyond what that person could imagine, but they must first have a repentant heart: they must be open and ready for change. To pray to receive Christ with someone who is not open to change is to do them a great disservice. Their prayer will be empty. They will not be saved.

The great revivalist, Charles G. Finney, wouldn't pray with people to receive Christ until repentance was evident. (I'm not speaking of doing penance, or any other works to try and earn one's salvation. Repentance and penance are two different things. One is scriptural, the other is not.) When Brother Finney saw that the people were under the Spirit's conviction, he would send them home to spend the evening in that conviction, not praying with them until the next day. It was said that you could hear the people's cries and screams all night long throughout the neighborhood. They allowed their hearts to be penetrated with the truth, yielding their lives to God. When these people came to the service the next day, they were saved. Their conversions were real and lasting.

If we are preaching the same gospel that the early church preached, it must include repentance. When people repent, they will receive.

7
Sin

W e've seen that the sinner cannot come to Christ without repentance: a change of heart and mind. Their changed, open heart puts them in position to receive a changed nature. The sinner doesn't repent for particular *acts* of sin, rather, he or she repents for a *life* of sin. God responds by graciously giving them a new life: a new nature. This is the essence of repentance for the sinner (the person who does not yet know Christ).

Repentance also has a place in the life of the believer.

First, it's important to note that once the believer repents for a life of sin, he or she should never have to do so again. They are now to conduct their life according to their new nature, never again needing a nature-transplant. Jesus excluded the righteous (saved people) from repenting for a life of sin.

> *I have not come to call the righteous but sinners to re-*
> *pentance.*
> *Luke 5:32*

Does that mean that the believer never has to repent for sin? No. However, their situation is the mirror image of the sinner's situation. The sinner doesn't repent for *acts* of sin, but rather for a *life* of sin, whereas the believer doesn't repent for a life of sin, but rather for individual acts of sin. Because of the believer's new nature, sin should be infrequent, and major repentance a rarity.

What if believers get away from God and go off into sin? They need to repent. They need to change.

Much needs to be said along these lines. Some have the idea that it's acceptable to stray from the things of God and pursue the desires of the flesh for a season. Some even teach that God is okay with sin, that He understands that we all have certain *needs* that must be met. They teach that He looks the other way and is always ready to take us back. We must be careful about twisted teachings such as these. Remember, it was Jesus Himself who threatened to remove the candlestick of the church that had drifted from Him. What does it mean to have your candlestick removed? I am not interested in finding out.

I have actually heard it taught in recent years that *God wants us to be happy, and if sex makes you happy, then God is okay with you having sex.* People who teach such things need to resign from ministry. Sex is only permissible within the male-female marriage union, period. Sex outside of marriage will ruin your life.

God is not a *come-and-go* God, where you serve Him one day, then take a break for several days, then come back, etc. True, He is exceedingly merciful, and gives many chances, but it's possible to exhaust His patience and grace. When a person knows better and has been taught the truth, they cannot just take a *vacation from God* without facing consequences. Sin *always* has consequences. Sin *always* leads to death. Listen to these ultra-strong words of Jesus along these lines:

> *But I have this against you, that you tolerate that woman Jezebel, who calls herself a prophetess and is teaching and seducing my servants to practice sexual immorality and to eat food sacrificed to idols.* ***I gave her time to repent****, but she refuses to repent of her sexual immorality. Behold, I will throw her onto a sickbed, and those who commit adultery with her I will throw into great tribulation,* **unless they repent** *of her works.*
>
> *Revelation 2:20-22*

Jesus spoke strongly while here on earth, but He never said anything quite this strong while on earth. Why the change in tone? Weren't the people He was ministering to on earth practicing some of these same sins? Perhaps. The difference was, they weren't yet born again. They hadn't been fully enlightened and empowered to resist sin. When a person knows better, he or she will be held accountable. This church knew better. They were compromising, and our sweet, gentle Jesus loved them enough to give them a tongue lashing. I pray they heeded His warning, repented, and thanked Him for His correction.

Notice in the above verses the connection between immorality and sickness. Those who are loose with their lifestyle will be unable to resist sickness when it comes to them. Before sleeping around, the believer might want to make sure that he or she has a good health insurance policy in place, for the Word of God gives us reason to believe that sickness will be imminent.

REPENT WHILE YOU CAN

*I gave her **time to repent**, but she does not want to turn away from her immorality.*

Revelation 2:21 (NLT)

When people don't want to turn from sin, God will allow them to harden themselves and suffer the consequences. Notice, however, that He doesn't just say *That's it!* and drop the hammer of judgement upon us. He gives us *time to repent*. Neither the original language, nor the context of this passage implies that this period of time is unlimited. On the contrary, it's very clearly speaking of a limited opportunity. The believer is wise to immediately take advantage of his or her opportunity to repent.

We are silly to play around with things like sin and think that all will be okay. We must respect God, the righteous judge, and we must respect the devil who steals, kills, and destroys. (When I speak of respecting the devil, I'm referring to being sober about the fact that he will take any opportunity he can to work destruction in our lives.) Some reason within themselves, *Well, I'll just do it, and then repent to God later.* Says who? Who says that you can repent whenever you want? Perhaps there's more about repentance that we don't yet understand.

*When they heard these things they fell silent. And they glorified God, saying, "Then to the Gentiles also God has **granted repentance** that leads to life."*

Acts 11:18

*Do you suppose, O man—you who judge those who practice such things and yet do them yourself—that you will escape the judgment of God? Or do you presume on the riches of his kindness and forbearance and patience, not knowing that God's kindness is meant to **lead you to repentance?***

Romans 2:3-4

*You have neither part nor lot in this matter, for your heart is not right before God. **Repent**, therefore, of this wickedness of yours, and pray to the Lord that, **if possible**, the intent of your heart may be forgiven you.*

Acts 8:21-22

We may make the decision to repent, but the *ability* to repent comes from God. He grants us repentance; leads us into repentance. A repentant heart is not a work of the flesh, but a work of the Spirit of God.

In order to sin, a person must harden their heart. If they continue to push past the warnings of God's Spirit, the day will come when their hardness of heart will prevail and they will not be able to repent. We are not to assume that when we deliberately move out into sin that we will be able to repent afterward. (Remember the story of Pharaoh, who withstood Moses too many times and saw his heart hardened, unable to change?) Let's renew our minds to both the kindness and the severity of God.

> *Note then the kindness and the severity of God: severity toward those who have fallen, but God's kindness to you, provided you continue in his kindness. Otherwise you too will be cut off.*
>
> *Romans 11:22*

The story of Esau, Jacob's brother, is one of the clearest examples we have of someone who waited too long to repent.

> *Look after each other so that none of you fails to receive the grace of God. Watch out that no poisonous root of bitterness grows up to trouble you, corrupting many. Make sure that no one is immoral or godless like Esau, who traded his birthright as the firstborn son for a single meal. You know that afterward, when he wanted his father's blessing, he was rejected. **It was too late for repentance, even though he begged with bitter tears.***
>
> *Hebrews 12:15-17 (NLT)*

Repentance can sometimes include tears, but tears are not the same as repentance. Crying alone won't get the job done. These are heart issues, not tear-duct issues. Repentance is a change of heart and is granted by God for a limited time. Always repent right away. Better yet, don't stray from Him in the first place. God loves you and has given you all the grace you need to live for Him and enjoy His victory.

We can see that those who teach that sin has already been taken care of, and that the believer never has to repent or confess, are misapplying certain scriptures while ignoring many others. Sin, at great cost, has indeed been taken care of, but it's so we can resist it, not embrace it.

There is a delicate balance to this truth. While believers should not be cavalier with sin, neither should they live in fear of missing it, being rejected, losing their salvation, or committing the sin unto death. God's grace is sufficient for us and will keep us. We are secure in Him. Although we don't live in fear, the believer should be afraid to purposely walk away from what they know, even for a minute. The believer who finds that they have sinned should repent – change – and should express that repentance in accordance with this great promise:

If we confess our sins, he is faithful and just to forgive us our sins and to cleanse us from all unrighteousness.

1 John 1:9

CONFESSION

The word *confess* is a very interesting word in the Greek language. It is the compound word *homologeo*. *Logeo* is a form of the word *logos* meaning *to speak* or *to say*. *Homo* means *the same*. To *confess* therefore means *to speak the same*. When we confess a sin, we go to God and say the same thing about it that He says. We agree with Him that it's wrong, get back on His side, and commit to never do it again. Confession is the vocal part of repentance. We verbalize with our mouths what's real in our heart.

As a believer, I have missed it at times and sinned. (I don't live conscious of the sins of my past because they no longer exist. The blood of Jesus has washed them away, praise God.) No one forced me to sin, I chose to. In every case, I had allowed my flesh to become stronger than my spirit. (When we don't keep ourselves spiritually strong, we yield to sin.)

I've missed it in big ways and in small ways. But I repented. Although I don't dwell on my now-cleansed past, I can remember times when I realized I had sinned. I fell on my face and cried my heart out before God. It broke my heart that I had broken His heart; that I had violated His Word, broke fellowship with Him, let Him down, and walked unworthy of His precious blood. I repented. At that particular moment, I abhorred myself, like Job. There was disappointment, tears, and intense heaviness. It was not fun, but it had to be done. I had to repent.

I confessed, agreed with God about the sin, and got up clean, purposing never again to transgress in that way. He forgave me and cleansed me from my sin, just as He said He would. Repenting for sin, as we have said, should be a rare occurrence in the life of the believer, but it is nevertheless part of the believer's life. Thank God for His grace and mercy. Thank God for repentance.

8

Make the Change

I remember the touching story of a great minister who came home from the doctor after being told that he had cancer. He sat down in a chair and began to talk to God about it, understanding that God wasn't the author of cancer, nor was He the one responsible for afflicting him. The Lord graciously showed him where he had opened the door to the enemy. It was not that he had committed some terrible act, rather, he had backed off of part of his ministry assignment, and failed to heed the Lord's warning to properly rest. (Sin is not always something dirty or evil. We can sin by failing to obey God fully, or by falling short of His plan for our lives.)

This minister immediately repented and broke down, crying before the Lord. He wasn't crying because of the doctor's report; they were tears of disappointment for having let down the one that he loved so much. He didn't argue or make excuses before the Lord, he just repented. There was a change of heart and mind before the Lord; a change of purpose and direction. As soon as he repented, the Lord spoke up and told him, *The cancer will be gone within 30 days*. It happened exactly as God said, and this man ministered on earth for many more years.

Notice again the connection between repenting and receiving. As soon as this man repented, he received. What if he had instead turned bitter toward God? What if he hadn't repented, or only gave the Lord a half-hearted response? The earth wouldn't have enjoyed this man's most effective years of ministry. Do we enjoy the process of repentance? Not so much, but if it's a choice between repentance and cancer, I'll take repentance every time.

We continue to see that the essence of repentance is change. Change can be dramatic, and repentance a heavy thing, but change can also be slight and repentance quick and easy. We are mistaken to see only the sackcloth-and-ashes side of repentance when there's also the every-day side: small changes and adjustments that must constantly be made in order to stay aligned with God. These changes keep us perpetually positioned to receive from Him.

Most people don't like change. They don't like admitting they are wrong. They prefer status quo, and do not appreciate the discomfort of having their routine interrupted. I understand these sentiments, for I have flesh like anyone else, and the flesh always wants to be in control. We must, however, overcome the flesh, for we simply cannot live for God without change. Change is a regular occurrence in the Christian's life.

New Dog, New Tricks

I once taught on some of these truths in the church that I pastored. After one service, an older lady came up to me and said, *You know, you can't teach an old dog new tricks.* (It's amazing how people will come up and argue with what was just preached from the Word of God, quoting worldly sayings as though they were Scripture.) Without thinking, I responded, *I thought the Word of God said you were a new creature, not an old dog.* She needed to renew her mind to this truth: we can change, if we will change.

This lady had a friend standing next to her who spoke up and said, *Well, some of us are just set in our ways.* You mean *set* like fast-setting concrete? No problem. There's a way to move concrete when you need to. You just break it. Sometimes, that's what needs to happen with us. We must have our old attitudes, our small thinking, and our hardness of heart broken up. Let go of those old ways and let God replace them with His ways.

A philosophy of avoiding change works for no one. I have lived in cities whose main industries began to be affected by shifts in the economy. Instead of being proactive with change, these cities dug in their heels and rode those industries into the ground. They finally went out of business. Now the city of several hundred thousand people is bankrupt, all because the people and government didn't want to face change. What must they do now? Now they are forced to change. Had they made the change when they first saw it coming it would have been easier and could have taken place gradually. Now the change is immediate, drastic, and painful.

Life is constantly changing. It's best to get on board with that fact. Change can sometimes be uncomfortable, but there's great news: God and His Word never changes. He is our constant. As long as I have the Lord, everything else around me can change, and I know I'll be okay.

There has been more than one time in my life when I have lost all of my income with no idea how to replace any of it. My bills, obligations, and needs still remained, but my income had disappeared. You talk about change! Everything around me had changed, but thankfully, nothing in me had changed. God was still my source. I was able to take great comfort in the fact that, although my income was gone, my divine supply was not. God took care of us in fine fashion. It's easier to be open to change when you know the Unchanging One.

ADJUSTMENTS

The believer who maintains a repentant heart will be able to successfully make the many changes that arise in life. There is one level of change that is almost constant. We could call these changes *adjustments*.

Remember, the definition of *repentance* is *a change of mind.* I am constantly adjusting my thinking, bringing it into alignment with the Word of God. Why? Because we can only receive from Him when we are properly aligned with Him. Throughout the day, I must be diligent to monitor my thoughts, words, and actions, bringing all into captivity to the obedience of Christ (2 Corinthians 10:5).

These constant adjustments should not be a foreign concept to us. Any of us who have ever driven an automobile know that adjustments are constantly taking place. It would be great if all we had to do was point our car in the direction we wanted to go, never having to steer, but it doesn't work that way. The entire time I am driving I am adjusting my wheel, keeping my car aligned with the road before me. We must do the same thing with God. Small, daily adjustments, conforming to His will, are the every-day level of repentance for which the believer is responsible.

Do you catch yourself talking about a situation with words of doubt instead of words of faith? Repent. In other words, just make the change. Don't do it later, do it right now. It's easy and it only takes a second. If you're speaking with someone, just say, *That's not what I meant to say, this is what I mean.* No sackcloth or ashes are needed for this kind of repentance. Just make the change and go on. These little heart-adjustments that we make keep us aligned with the Word of God, enabling Him to bring His power and help to our life. Make the change, receive God's help. No change, no help.

COURSE CORRECTIONS

When an airplane gets just a little bit off course, it's no big deal, provided that the correction is quickly made. If a correction is not made, however, that small error in navigation can lead to a major detour. The pilot would need to make a definite course correction so that the flight to Houston doesn't end up in Havana. Yes, the plane is still going south – the intended direction – but the results weren't quite as planned, and the detour made it take a little longer to get there.

Just like that airplane, it's possible for the believer to find themselves off course. No, they're not backslidden or participating in evil, they have simply allowed themselves to veer off to some degree. A minister who influenced me greatly tells of one such time in his ministry. He had been preaching for almost fifty years when the Lord dealt with him that he had gotten off course in one area of his ministry.

The Lord had instructed this minister to open a healing center, which he had done. Along with ministering healing, this minister offered counseling services to people who needed help with their problems. The Lord spoke to this minister and said, *I never told you to counsel people. People need to be counseled in their own sheepfold* (church). I'm glad to say that this minister repented and made the correction immediately. Just like that, the counseling stopped. He made the change – a course correction – and things again began to work wonderfully.

In this man's case there was no sin (in the sense of doing something bad), yet it wasn't God's plan. He was expending *empty energy* in that part of his ministry. In the right setting, counseling can be a good thing, but this just wasn't the right setting. Again, just because it's a good thing doesn't mean it's a God-thing.

It's certainly possible for the believer to never veer off course, yet most of us will have at least a few course corrections in life. Learning to navigate the leadings of the Spirit and growing in our knowledge of the Word will help us stay on course, progressing in the plan of God.

Another minister tells of the time that he purchased a car that he believed God was leading him to buy. The only problem was, he didn't yet know the difference between the leadings of the Spirit and the lusts of his flesh. He bought that car and everything about it was wrong. It had mechanical trouble that it shouldn't have had, he couldn't make the payments when they were due, and most importantly, he couldn't tithe and give like he knew he was supposed to. It certainly wasn't *the blessing of the Lord with no sorrow added* (Proverbs 10:22).

This wasn't just a minor, daily adjustment for this minister, it was a course correction. Getting out of a newly-purchased vehicle is not always easy, and money is often lost. Thankfully, God is merciful. This man repented and got rid of the car. He made the change and got back on-course. He also learned to pay better attention to the leadings of the Spirit. Eventually, the Lord did lead him into a beautiful new vehicle.

I sometimes tell the story of the lawn tractor that I purchased several years ago. A friend of mine had been loaning me his older tractor that he wasn't using. (I think I was actually doing him a favor by getting it out of his garage.) Although he never told me he needed it back, I decided that I had kept it long enough, and that I needed a newer one that would be more reliable, make a nicer cut, etc.

Understand this: God doesn't mind you or me having a new lawn tractor if we want one or need one. However, it matters that we are led by Him, following His timing. I knew God was okay with me having one, but since I knew He was on board with the *what,* I decided that I would go ahead and determine the *when,* and that the *when* would be *right now.*

I purchased that tractor using a credit card, because I knew I would have the cash to pay it off in just a few weeks. (I couldn't wait, after all; the grass was growing fast and I certainly didn't want to use any of the other mowers already in my garage.) You can guess what happened. For some reason, the money that I was supposed to receive never showed up, and there I was with a new tractor and a huge credit card bill. I did enjoy that tractor, but only for about one or two seasons before the Lord led us to move out of the area. I had to sell it for a loss.

When I saw that I had missed it, I repented. I made the heart-change, confessed to the Lord, and went on. I also learned a valuable lesson. Every time I contemplate buying something and begin to think, *I don't need to bother seeking the Lord about this little thing,* I remember the tractor and take time to check my heart. (I also remember how difficult it was to pay off that credit card.) That tractor helped me realize that if God's not in it, I don't want it. Let's become experts at listening to God and staying on course. If we find that we have gotten off, we should quickly repent and make the change.

U-TURNS

We've all done it. We were supposed to exit the highway at exit 324B, but we took exit 324A instead. Now, instead of going south, we are headed north. (It's always nice to discover this kind

of mistake before traveling two hours in the wrong direction.)
What do you do? The only thing you can: make a U-turn and
start going in the right direction.

It's possible for a Christian to be going the wrong direction.
Although it should never happen in the believer's life, it does
happen to people every day. They get off God's path by taking
an exit that He never intended, and end up in great difficulty.
God has provided many safeguards in our life to help keep us on
course. The believer must override them all to end up going the
wrong direction.

People move to places that God didn't direct them to, take
jobs He didn't tell them to, marry people He didn't lead them to,
and start ministries He never asked them to. Just as bad, is when
people leave the church and pastor that God had joined them to.
These things aren't just slight detours, they are wrong directions,
and the results can be disastrous. These kinds of decisions are
how you lose your children, lose your house, lose your business,
and lose your life. Life gets real bumpy when you leave God's
highway, forcing the whole family to go off-roading.

If you have gone the wrong direction, God is not condemning
you. He still loves you and wants to help you get back on course.
However, you're going to have to repent, make a U-turn, and
head back to the last thing He told you to do.

Did you leave the church in which He planted you? Repent
and return. Did you start a ministry you weren't directed to? Repent, ask the Lord what He wants you to do with it, and follow
through in obedience. *Yes, but I've worked twenty years on this.* I

know. But twenty-one years isn't going to magically turn it into the will of God. You must repent and make the change. I know it might be a heavy thing to admit that you've been this far off for so long, but you must do it. Mean it. Lay your heart before God. Wait on Him until you're clear as to what He would have you do. He's not mad at you. He wants to help you, but He needs your repentance.

I have a dear friend who was raised in the things of God, but went the wrong direction in life. It was no one's fault but his own. This man was arrested for armed robbery and spent time in jail. He actually escaped from prison and was running for his life when God arrested him, spoke to his heart, and told him that he was receiving his last opportunity to get right. He repented right there and surrendered his life to God. No one was with him except the Lord. His repentance was genuine; his experience real.

You talk about a U-turn. What do you do when you're supposed to be behind bars but you're not? The Lord instructed him to go turn himself in. He was facing a life-without-parole sentence. Now what? Only God could turn this man's hopeless situation around. Days turned into weeks, and then months, but because this man maintained a repentant heart, he ended up being released even after the parole board said it would never happen. Eventually, he received a full pardon. This man has been in ministry, blessing the Body of Christ for decades, all because he made the change.

Repentance aligns our life with God. When a person has been moving in a direction opposite of God, it can sometimes take a while to get things turned around (the way it takes more time and space for an ocean liner to turn around than it does for a jet ski). The important thing is to get pointed in the right direction. When repentance is in place, God can do amazing things. You may think that you will have to drive all the way back to where you took the wrong exit, but with God you can look up to find a newly constructed on-ramp, right where you are.

Remember, God sees the heart and responds to the repentant heart. It is true, there are some situations and consequences that are not easily changed, but don't think that you are disqualified from having God's best. If you have repented, you can have God's best from this point on. What He will do for you will amaze you.

Whether we're speaking of U-turns, course corrections, or minor every-day adjustments, God is big enough to take us all the way to victory. The only limit to what He can do are the limits that He finds within us. If we will fully repent, laying our hearts wide-open before Him, He is able to do the impossible. He just can't do it without us. We must make the change.

9

Make It Right

---

*And he said, "There was a man who had two sons. And the younger of them said to his father, 'Father, give me the share of property that is coming to me.' And he divided his property between them. Not many days later, the younger son gathered all he had and took a journey into a far country, and there he squandered his property in reckless living. And when he had spent everything, a severe famine arose in that country, and he began to be in need. So he went and hired himself out to one of the citizens of that country, who sent him into his fields to feed pigs. And he was longing to be fed with the pods that the pigs ate, and no one gave him anything. "But **when he came to himself**, he said, 'How many of my father's hired servants have more than enough bread, but I perish here with hunger! I will arise and go to my father, and I will say to him, "Father, I have sinned against heaven and before you. I am no longer worthy to be called your son. Treat me as one of your hired servants."' And he arose and came to his father. But while he was still a long way off, his father saw him and felt compassion, and ran and embraced him and kissed him. And the son said to him,*

'Father, I have sinned against heaven and before you. I am no longer worthy to be called your son.' But the father said to his servants, 'Bring quickly the best robe, and put it on him, and put a ring on his hand, and shoes on his feet. And bring the fattened calf and kill it, and let us eat and celebrate. For this my son was dead, and is alive again; he was lost, and is found.' And they began to celebrate.

Luke 15:11-24

This story shows not only the unconditional love that our Father has for us, it also shows repentance in action. Repentance was granted to this young man, enabling him to *come to himself*. The boy saw what he had done, recognized his stupidity, and repented. He didn't just repent to the Lord, however. He made it his priority to also express repentance to the person who was most affected by his sin: his father.

I will arise and go to my father, and I will say to him, "Father, I have sinned against heaven and before you."

Luke 15:18

REPENTING TO OTHERS

Repentance – a change of mind – can often involve people other than the Lord. When a believer sins, gets off course, etc., it's common that others have been affected by their actions. In such cases, repenting before the Lord may not be enough. That person must go to the Lord, and also to the person (or people) that were wronged.

Repenting to others can be particularly difficult for some people. If a person finds that repenting or apologizing to others is hard, it likely indicates that their heart is hard. The flesh hates to lower itself before others, but that's exactly what must happen at times. There is no way around this for the believer. Everyone will have at least a few times where they end up saying or doing something that negatively affects another person. All of us must learn to repent to others.

Learning to repent to other people is sort of like learning to jump into the deep end of a swimming pool. There's really no easy way to do it other than just jumping in. It may be uncomfortable, but once it's done, you're glad you did it.

True repentance doesn't stop until the job is done. Saying you confessed to the Lord, but failing to come before the person you wronged is not full repentance, and it's not something God can honor. Many people regret what they said or did, but regret alone is not repentance. Repentance follows through. It makes the change, and it *makes it right*.

*And Zacchaeus stood and said to the Lord, "Behold, Lord, the half of my goods I give to the poor. **And if I have defrauded anyone of anything, I restore it four-***

fold." *And Jesus said to him, "Today salvation has come to this house, since he also is a son of Abraham. For the Son of Man came to seek and to save the lost." Luke 19:8-10*

When Zaccheaus came to Jesus, he didn't just fill out a decision card and continue on with his life as a swindler. His major change of heart before God led him to change his actions before man. What he committed to restore to those he wronged could have bankrupted him. He didn't care. He had made the change and now wanted to make it right. The repentant heart knows that the price of keeping a transgression on one's conscience is much greater than any financial cost.

A Clear Conscience

Some years ago, I was involved in a business transaction with a man who promised to make a large donation to my ministry as part of the deal. The minister who introduced me to this man was promised the same donation to his ministry for any deals he arranged. Because I ended up dealing directly with this businessman instead of going through my minister friend, the money was promised to me. It was really an oversight on the businessman's part to have promised the same money to two different people.

I went through with the transaction and all went well with the deal. However, when the minister found out that my ministry was to receive the donation instead of his, he became very upset. He thought that I had gone behind his back to secure the donation. I can see how he would have thought that, however, I was not aware of their arrangement. It was a huge mess.

I didn't want this minister hurt, nor did I want my name to leave a bad taste in his mouth, so I repented to him. My repentance included yielding up the money that he felt was rightfully his. Repentance that day cost me tens of thousands of dollars, but it was worth it to be able to lay down to sleep that night with a clear conscience. I had to make the change, and I had to make it right. God has more than made up that money to me, but He wouldn't have been able to bring it to me had I not passed that test and repented.

> *Therefore I always exercise and discipline myself [mortifying my body, deadening my carnal affections, bodily appetites, and worldly desires, endeavoring in all respects] to have **a clear (unshaken, blameless) conscience, void of offense toward God and toward men.***
> *Acts 24:16 (AMP)*

Did I want to give up that money? Goodness no. When I thought about doing it, things came alive in me that I didn't realize were in me, but I had to put those thoughts and feelings down. I had to do some *mortifying* and *deadening*. Was it worth it? Yes. It was so worth it. Pay any price you have to pay to do the right thing and stay in peace.

PUBLIC REPENTANCE

And looking intently at the council, Paul said, "Brothers, I have lived my life before God in all good conscience up to this day." And the high priest Ananias commanded those who stood by him to strike him on the mouth. Then Paul said to him, "God is going to strike you, you whitewashed wall! Are you sitting to judge me according to the law, and yet contrary to the law you order me to be struck?" Those who stood by said, "Would you revile God's high priest?" And Paul said, "I did not know, brothers, that he was the high priest, for it is written, You shall not speak evil of a ruler of your people."'

Acts 23:1-5

It's one thing to act repentant when you get caught doing something you weren't supposed to, or when you know you were just plain wrong. But what about when you really weren't at fault? What about when there's a room full of people watching? This story of the Apostle Paul standing up for the gospel in front of the hostile Sanhedrin council is inspiring, but even more inspiring is his response when the situation turned ugly.

And looking intently at the council, Paul said, "Brothers, I have lived my life before God in all good conscience up to this day." And the high priest Ananias commanded *those who stood by him to **strike him on the mouth.***

Acts 23:1-2

Paul spoke before the council with boldness and confidence. That kind of talk is great in some settings but not in a religious setting. Religion hates boldness and will slap a person down into unworthiness who dares declare that they are anything but a worm of the dust before God. Religion always seeks to bind and control its adherents. Truth, on the other hand, liberates and sets people free.

Have you ever been punched in the mouth? Whether it happened accidentally or on purpose, anyone who has ever been hit can testify that a smack in the face affects more than just the face. Pain and adrenalin kicks in, sending all reasonable thoughts to the background. That's why we sometimes see one little guy taking on a whole gang by himself. Someone smacked him in the mouth and all good sense flew out the window.

No one can fault Paul for responding the way he did. He was actually correct, they were hitting him against the law. His response, however, brought a collective gasp to the room. He was informed that the person he had just rebuked was the high priest. Perhaps the priest was summoned to this hearing hastily and hadn't had time to put on his priestly garments. In any case, Paul did not recognize the person to whom he was speaking.

His mouth must have still been throbbing, maybe even oozing with blood. However, when told that he had just rebuked the high priest, he apologized – repented – right there in front of everyone. The high priest's office was a place worthy of honor – even when being abused – and Paul backed off and backed down, trusting instead in God's ability to vindicate. What a tremendous show of honor. What an amazing heart he had. He made a U-turn right there in the council chamber and repented, when he really wasn't guilty of anything. Is it any wonder Paul was able to receive so much from God? He knew how to receive, because he knew how to repent.

Repentance is not fun, and public repentance is sure not fun. I have watched when high-profile leaders have fallen, and I've seen their public apologies. There's nothing pleasant about the whole scene. It's obvious that some were truly repentant, and some were just sorry: sorry that they got caught.

The world is ruthless when a leader falls. They, of course, don't know the scripture that tells us to *restore, considering ourselves, lest we also be tempted* (Galatians 6:1). The world loves to sit in judgement and make a leader repent over and over. That's not godly. When repentance is genuine, forgiveness from heaven comes quickly. Although there may be consequences to suffer, it's not necessary to keep a sour, heavy look on one's face perpetually.

It's my heartfelt desire never to find myself in a position where I have violated the trust of the people I am serving. I want to finish my race here on earth having been as faithful as possible. While it's true that neither I nor anyone else ever has to fall, it's also likely that mistakes will happen here and there. (Remember, leaders aren't just responsible for their own mistakes, but also sometimes for the mistakes of people who represent them in different capacities.)

There was a time when I was pastoring when I felt it necessary to publicly repent to my church. (No, I didn't cheat on my wife or steal anyone's money, but there are other situations where repentance is appropriate.) A couple had just left our church the week before because of a sermon I had preached that they felt was insensitive. The other people in my church did not even know this family had left.

They were correct, I was insensitive. I had been helping another minister with some meetings the entire week before and had little time to get quiet and pray about my weekend service. This couple in our church had been through a very traumatic situation and had missed a few weeks of church while getting their feet back under them. This particular Sunday was their first week back in a while. The message that I preached on hearing from God was meant to be good news, but parts of it could have been taken as a rebuke, pouring salt into their wounds. Although that was not my intention, that's what happened.

What I preached was truth, but had I taken time to pray more about the service, I'm sure that the Spirit would have, at the very least, cautioned me about my delivery. I know I could have avoided hurting this couple at a time when they needed healing.

I felt horribly about what had happened and repented before the Lord. I made the change. Then I got in touch with this couple and repented for hurting them. As much as I could, I made it right. Lastly, I felt as though I should apologize to my whole congregation, which I did the following week.

It's not always necessary to take things public, but I was led to in this situation. Ours was a smaller church and these people had been leaders in the church. People would notice that they were gone and would soon begin to talk, asking where they were, etc. It was best for me to address this head-on.

I simply told the congregation what had happened and apologized to them for hurting a member of our church family. I was genuine, honest, and brief, and then I moved on. People came to me after the service and said they had never seen a minister do that before. Believe me, I didn't look forward to it, and didn't want to have to do it. But it needed to happen. I had already repented several times over the last few days; I could handle one more time.

It didn't occur to me until later that it's important for ministers to set the example of repentance in their church. In the same way, husbands and wives should set the example of repentance in the home. If you fuss and fight in front of the kids, repent and make up in front of them. (I understand that some things might need to be discussed in private.)

Making It Right in the Home

I have snapped at my wife before in front of my kids. If my kids saw and heard that, then they need to be in on the repentance. Everybody gets in on it: first God, then my wife, then my kids.

We have trained our kids to look to our example in the home of how a married couple treats each other. If I deviate from that example and don't repent to them, it tells them that my wrong behavior was okay.

Have you ever apologized to your kids? Have you ever apologized to your spouse? If you haven't, you need to, right now. Repent for going all this time and never apologizing. (We know you haven't been perfect all these years.) You'll be amazed at what happens.

When I repented to my church, it did something to my church. It made the connection of the people to the church stronger. When I have repented to my wife or kids, it didn't weaken our family, it strengthened it. There have been times when my wife and I have repented to each other. That's not a bad thing, it's a beautiful thing. We were able to receive from each other again. We had revival right there in our bedroom!

Because repentance is uncomfortable, people often do nothing after an ugly situation. That's easiest on the flesh, but it can ruin a relationship. Do not use silence as a substitute for repentance. Although your silence may at other times be appreciated, it's not okay to just go about, acting as though nothing happened.

There is one whose rash words are like sword thrusts, but the tongue of the wise brings healing.

Proverbs 12:18

Don't leave an open wound in someone when you, and only you, can bring healing to that person. Be a man. Be a woman. Take the lead in repentance. Make the change. Make it right.

10
Repent and Be Healed

Rev. Kenneth E. Hagin used to tell the story about a lady in one of his churches who asked him why her family members never seemed to receive healing, but her husband's family always seemed to receive healing. She noted that her family was the more faithful, more spiritual family, which made the issue all the more confusing to her.

Brother Hagin said he couldn't specifically answer her question unless the Lord were to reveal the reasons, but that he could answer her in a general manner. He said there were three characteristics that must have been prominent in her husband's family for them to regularly receive the help they needed: they must have been quick to forgive, quick to believe, and quick to repent.

This lady looked at Brother Hagin like he had just read her mind. He had perfectly described her in-laws. Although they weren't the *more spiritual family*, they were the family that was quickest to repent. (News flash: being quick to repent is actually more spiritual than being slow to repent.) The believer who wants to receive help from the Lord in time of need or trouble must be quick to repent. Just like we would counsel the lost person not to wait to decide to follow Christ, the saved person should immediately turn from sin when it occurs, and repent.

Sin separates, but repentance restores. Remember that God never changes. It's not that He gets mad and turns away from us. Our sin moves us away from Him. Yes, we are still part of His family, but are at odds with Him; out of fellowship; out of alignment. The change that occurs when we repent restores our fellowship with Him, and restores the flow of His power toward us.

I have known people who found themselves in a dire physical situation, needing healing. Before their body could change, however, there had to be a heart-change. In some cases, the person had been opposed to the message of faith and healing. Now they needed both, but had none. The only answer was for them to make the change. Some did just that and received. Others, because of years of religious tradition, remained opposed to the Word and died.

Some might say, *Well, it just wasn't God's sovereign will to heal them.* God had nothing to do with it. The person never made the change that would have aligned their life with God's power.

AGREE AND ALIGN

Agree with God, and be at peace; thereby good will come to you.

Job 22:21

I think some people read that verse and must have thought the word *agree* was really the word *argue*. Those words may share some of the same letters, but they are not the same word.

How does one agree with God? Receive what He's said and say, *Amen. Yes sir. I agree.* We are not to respond to God's Word with excuses, reasons why it won't work, etc. Stop arguing and start agreeing, and you'll have His help. When the Word of God goes against your thinking or the direction of your life, repent – come into agreement – and make the change.

It's amazing how many people would rather argue than agree. They would rather do without than change what they think. They would rather die than agree with God about healing. They would rather starve than tithe and agree with God about prosperity. They would sooner divorce than agree that they are the problem in their marriage. They would lose everything before getting on their face before God, making it right with other people, and repenting. Repentance is foundational to our life. Agree with God! Repent!

Brother Hagin tells of the time when he was preaching in a certain town, and another minister in that town was preaching against him and his meetings. Soon after, that man had a medical event occur in his life that could have easily been fatal. The Lord spoke to him and said, *I'll heal you if you'll repent for speaking against Brother Hagin.* In order to be healed, this man had to ask Brother Hagin to forgive him, his congregation to forgive him, and all the congregations from the surrounding churches who participated in the meetings to forgive him. This man went on a repentance tour. Then he had to get Brother Hagin to lay hands on him. That's some serious repenting, but it sure beats dying.

People think that the power of God is what's needed for their healing. They are correct, but so many times there's something in between them and the power of God. What they think is a power issue may really be a forgiveness issue, or a love-walk issue, or a watch-what-comes-out-of-your-mouth issue. You'll have to come clean to your spouse about that little secret (or that big secret). You'll have to obey God and stop eating what He told you not to eat. You'll have to send the money He told you to send to that preacher. No, not to earn or buy your healing, but to align yourself with Him so that His power can flow in your life and drive out the work of the devil.

Healing is connected to the many other areas of our life. We should not only focus on prayer or faith, but also on the other issues that may be preventing us from receiving our help. Truly, healing is often spelled R-E-P-E-N-T.

11

Refreshing

Repent therefore, and turn back, that your sins may be blotted out, that times of refreshing may come from the presence of the Lord, and that he may send the Christ appointed for you, Jesus, whom heaven must receive until the time for restoring all the things about which God spoke by the mouth of his holy prophets long ago.

Acts 3:19-21

No passage of Scripture conveys the theme of this book more clearly than this one. In it, we see a picture of how we are to progress toward the end of our age. Although this passage (part of Peter's sermon following the healing of the crippled man at the temple gate) was originally spoken to sinners, it speaks strongly to the believer as well.

Where are we in the plan of God? We are presently in the Church Age, a period that will end when Christ returns. We know some of the events that will take place in the ages that follow, but we know very little compared to what we know about our present age. There's a reason for that. God needs us focused on the here-and-now rather than the hereafter. Many aspects of the future ages are out of our hands, but right now, we're totally hands-on.

This passage gives us a simple overview of the events leading to the end of our age. Let's explore these, starting with the last event, and working our way back to the present.

That he may send the Christ appointed for you, Jesus.

The return of Christ for His Church will mark the end of our age. This event is the goal-line on God's playing field. It's what all history is moving toward. His return is not just an isolated event on heaven's calendar, however. His return is connected to, and dependent upon, other events. This passage in Acts chapter three (as well as other passages) describes some of these events.

The time for restoring.

Christ is waiting in heaven until *the time for restoring* (or, *the restoration of all things,* as other translations render it). If His return is contingent upon this restoration, it's obviously of great importance. In order to understand what this restoration is referring to, one must continue to read through this passage. We receive one clue right at the end of verse 21: *which God spoke by the mouth of his holy prophets long ago.* This restoration is something that has been prophesied and spoken of for centuries: a major Biblical theme.

A restoration is something that has been brought back from a deteriorated state to a new condition. Since this restoration was prophesied long ago, the deterioration must also have occurred long ago. What does the Bible speak of that was so decayed that it needed to be completely renewed? The heart of man. All that Adam lost. Man's ability to commune with God, act like God, talk like God, live on God's level, and spread God's kingdom. God had created man *in His image, and in His likeness* (Genesis 1:26), but when Adam sinned, he died spiritually. Everything that had made man like God was compromised.

In Jesus, all that was lost by Adam has been restored. Today, we are new creatures in Christ. Our spirits have been recreated. God lives within us and has made us joint-heirs: equal partners with Christ. God now has a Body on earth (the Church) capable of moving and flowing with Him, working with Him to accomplish the miraculous. The fullness of the Church Age – believers filled with God and flowing with His power – is what the Bible is referring to when it speaks of the *restoration of all things.*

The facts concerning this restoration are indisputable. However, we don't always see Christ's Body flowing with God as described above. That's because His Body doesn't know about their restoration as they should. Although this restoration is available *potentially*, it has not been known *experientially*. We have it, yet we don't often see it. (Similar to the difference between money in the bank and money in your pocket. It's all yours, but you can't experience, or spend, your money until it's in your possession.) Not until we make the change, seeing ourselves as who He says we are, will we experience the fullness of our restoration.

*And all the prophets who have spoken, from Samuel and those who came after him, also proclaimed **these days**.*

Acts 3:24

Many scholars believe that the *restoration of all things* is a reference to the Millennial Reign of Christ and the renovation of the Earth that follows. While it's true that the Earth awaits a much needed renovation, that's not the subject of this passage. Peter, speaking of this restoration, said it was prophesied for *these days*: a reference to the present Church Age. As the Church cooperates with God, we will experience this restoration: the full flow of God's power.

Power Restored

I have lived in areas where winter storms can cause severe damage and major inconvenience. When too much snow gets on power lines, for example, those lines can break and power can be lost for days. When the power is out, everybody goes into camping mode. For us, that meant moving over to my father-in-law's house. Our house had a heating source that required electricity to operate, but my father-in-law had a wood stove that would heat the entire house. When power is out in the winter, go where the heat is.

How primitive life became when there was no power. No internet, no television, no way to charge the cell phone. No lights other than candles, and no electric kitchen appliances. It was like we were living in early pioneer days. It's difficult to describe how wonderful it was when the power finally came back on. We would say that *power was restored.*

When power was restored, we were able to live life much more efficiently. No need to put a kettle of water on the stove, just heat it in the microwave. We could now see what we were doing in the bathroom. We could finally open the garage door to get our car out. Power changes everything.

During one outage, after power had been restored at my father-in-law's, we left to go back home. When we got back to our house, our neighbors told us that our power had only been out for an hour or two, not for the several days we were away. We stayed away that whole time because we didn't know what had been restored to us. We were ignorant that a restoration of power had taken place.

As the Church, we have had power restored to us. Nothing has been withheld. Nevertheless, many people are content to live as though we are in the spiritual dark ages. Too many tolerate ignorance in their lives and are satisfied with just a trickle of power here and there. Let's understand all that's been restored to us, taking advantage of the power that's ours. Let's tell the sinner that provision has been made for their restoration as well. I'm thankful that power has been restored.

The *restoration of all things* means that everything God has ever done – every act of power, every gift of the Spirit, every expression of love and compassion, every miracle of healing and provision – is flowing fully: working at full potential. There's no reason why we can't see this on the earth today. In fact, for Christ to return, we *must* see this on the earth. He waits in heaven for His Body to act like the mighty Church that they are.

Let's continue our look-in-reverse at the key parts of this passage.

Times of refreshing from the presence of the Lord.

The *times of refreshing* spoken of here are part of our power restoration. Prior to the return of Christ, there must be a great outpouring of God's presence (referred to elsewhere in Scripture as the *outpouring of His Spirit*, or *the rain*). The rain of God's Spirit contains all the gifts and manifestations of the Spirit: a strong flow of His power and presence. The presence of the Lord in manifestation is the move of God that we've been speaking of throughout this book.

In summarizing the events of the end of our age, Peter emphasized *times* (or seasons) *of refreshing*. *Refreshing* means *reviving with fresh air*. The Greek word used here could just as easily be translated *reviving* or *revival*.

Seasons of revival because of the presence of the Lord. I'll take it. I want it. This is what we're hungry for. We've experienced some of these seasons throughout the years, but it's time for a prolonged, intense season of revival to push us toward the end of our age.

Embracing the Outpouring

The end-time revival includes an outpouring of spiritual refreshing. Indeed, one of the waves of revival that the Lord has been endeavoring to bring the Body of Christ into is an outpouring of divine joy and refreshment. When the joy of the Lord is poured out, people respond with a variety of manifestations and expressions. Some of these (laughing, dancing, shouting, running, etc.) create controversy, as many people consider them to be undignified, not suitable for a church setting. A great many people have voiced their criticism about this kind of outpouring, calling it unnecessary, silly, and even demonic.

Our critics are correct about one thing: the move of God is not always dignified. Deliverance, healing, and freedom are not always neatly packaged. Sometimes the chairs have to be rearranged and the paint touched up after God moves in a service. Although we do endeavor to be people of dignity, reverence, and order (rather than being casual and unorganized), we are quick to change our outward posture to match the Spirit's movement. We want these times of refreshing. We desire seasons of revival. If we dismiss times of refreshing, we delay the coming of the Lord. The two are connected.

The movement of God's Spirit – any movement – is worthy of our reverence and embrace. We do not dismiss anything that God does based on our limited reasoning. Just because the purposes of certain types of services may not be evident does not mean that no purpose exists. The purposes of an outpouring of joy and refreshment are many, and they are great. One purpose is for Christ's Body to learn to flow and act together – putting aside the flesh – making the change to flow with God.

We will say more about this revival in a moment, but first let's summarize the progression that we have seen in this passage so far:

1. Jesus is coming back.

2. His return requires a restoration of the things of God: an outpouring that includes times of refreshing from His presence.

How easy is that? God pours out His Spirit, power is restored, and Jesus comes back.

Not so fast.

Our Part

None of this happens without us. (That's right, none of it.) That which God does in the earth is largely done through His Body. We, Christ's Body, must be involved and engaged, flowing with Him. We must continually align ourselves with His purposes if His plan is to come to pass. We must constantly make movement along with Him, making changes and adjustments as necessary. We must do what the first part of Acts 3:19 says: *repent therefore and turn back.*

Although this passage mentions turning from sins, it would

also include turning from those things that lead to sin, namely, our own thoughts, desires, and actions. (These things are more the issue for the committed believer than sinful behavior.) We must turn from our own ways in order to match His ways. For the believer, this is repentance in action.

The believer could apply this passage to his or her life by reading it this way: *Make the change to align with God. Then revival will come. . . .* If we will change and align with Him, *then* times of refreshing will be experienced, then the restoration of all things will be manifest, then the harvest will be reaped, and then Christ can return. Notice how verse 19 reads in the Wuest translation:

> *Therefore repent at once, **instantly changing your attitude**, and perform a right-about-face in order that your sins may be obliterated, in order that there may come epoch-making periods of spiritual revival and refreshment from the presence of the Lord.*

We are to change in order that revival may come. First we change, *then* we experience the outpouring that God has for us. Repentance and revival.

I believe this area is the Body of Christ's area of greatest deficiency. As a body, we often fail to keep step with God's movement. We come together to meet with God, yet when He moves among us, we either fail to recognize it, or refuse to respond. We too often fail to adapt, adjust, or course-correct in order to go His way. We default to the same patterns of worship that we have been used to. This might not seem like a big deal, but our failure to make these changes, insignificant as they may seem, is costing us big-time. It's costing us precious time and precious souls.

I have been in services where God initiated powerful movement. His presence was heavy in the room and waves of joy began to flow among the congregation. Yet, relatively few people responded to His movement. The result was similar to what would happen if a person threw a five-gallon bucket of water on a campfire that was just beginning to flame. That part of the service quickly died out, everyone breathing a collective sigh of relief as if to say, *Thank God we got that over with.*

What many don't realize, however, is that other things may have been connected to that movement. Had everyone made the change to enter in and participate, what other great things might have happened? What manifestations of healing would have taken place? What life-altering words of prophecy would have been spoken? Might this have been the wave that carried us out into deeper waters? Were there levels of power just ahead that would have thrust the church into revival and spread the knowledge of God throughout the community? When people quench the flow of God because they do not want to be bothered with change, these questions go unanswered.

Do not quench (suppress or subdue) the [Holy] Spirit.
1 Thessalonians 5:19 (AMP)

The move of God is all about moving with Him. It's all about making changes and adjustments in order to match His movement. If He leads us into exuberance, we joyfully respond. If He moves us to reverent silence, we quietly melt in His presence. Whichever way He moves is the way we are to move. We make the change to follow His movement.

Change is the essence of repentance. Repentance is an integral part of revival. There's no revival without repentance, because God can't move all by Himself.

Let's finish the list we started earlier:

1. Jesus is coming back.

2. His return requires a restoration of the things of God: an outpouring that includes times of refreshing from His presence.

3. To experience this outpouring, the Church must have a repentant heart: willing to change, align with His purposes, and flow with Him.

This book is called *Repentance and Revival* because those two words go together (just as repentance and receiving go together). Revival is not just about us begging God to send something down from heaven. He must indeed do His part, but we must also do our part. He's waiting for us to repent, respond, and receive what heaven has made available. He's waiting for us to make the change.

12

Equipped for the Era

The revival that God desires for us consists of more than people getting excited and running around the room. There are
miracles, divine encounters, and signs and wonders in this revival. There's also a mighty harvest of souls that must be reaped (the
ultimate purpose of any revival is the salvation of the lost). It will
take the supernatural power of God – the revival in full force –
to reap this great harvest.

How exactly will we reap this harvest? What does it look like?
Will there be stadiums full of people seeking God? People meeting one-on-one in homes and coffee shops? Standing-room only
in the local churches? New churches being planted? Bible studies in the workplace? Yes. All of the above. Seasoned ministers
will be needed to stand at the forefront and lead, but they won't
do everything. Believers everywhere will be involved, doing the
works of God.

So I ask again, how? How will the Christian do their part to
reap the harvest? Many people think, *I don't know, we just will.*
Well, we haven't up until now, so what's going to change?

Equipped

The only way believers will be able to reap the harvest is if they are *equipped* to reap the harvest. I'm not just speaking of natural training, such as what to say when witnessing to someone, I'm referring to being spiritually equipped. The spiritually equipped believer must have a working knowledge of the Word of God. They must also develop enough spiritual sensitivity to be able to flow with God, making movement with Him.

How does the believer learn the ways of the Spirit? How does one learn the movement of God? There are several areas of training to which the believer must submit, some being more obvious than others. As we have already indicated, the follower of Christ must learn what Christ has said. He or she must be a student of the Word.

The believer must also develop his or her spirit by praying in the spirit. Much time (not just a little time, but much time) should be spent praying, speaking, and singing in other tongues. Speaking in tongues requires the believer to quiet their mind and yield to the utterances of the Spirit within them. This practice contributes greatly to the believer's spiritual development. There is no substitute for time spent praying in other tongues.

As one learns the Word and prays in the spirit, they can be effectively led by the Spirit. The Spirit's leadings through life are not meant to be random and obscure, but rather distinct and dependable. We can be led to speak to a person about Christ, minister to the sick, etc. in the same way that we are led in our every-day personal decisions.

Serving in the ministry of helps in the local church is another area that helps equip the believer to flow with God. How so? Natural jobs done in a spiritual setting require spiritual skills. When you do things for God, you don't just do as you please, you do it to please Him. You may be asked to do a job in the church differently than you would do it at home. These instructions aren't restrictive, they are meant to help develop flexibility and a willing heart. The local church is the place that knocks you out of your natural routine and requires you to adapt and adjust. These skills help the believer flow with God.

WAITING ON GOD

We spoke in a previous chapter of the different types of prayer. One type of prayer that the believer is to practice is what could be called *waiting upon the Lord*.

> *But they that wait upon the Lord shall renew their strength; they shall mount up with wings as eagles; they shall run, and not be weary; and they shall walk, and not faint.*
>
> Isaiah 40:31 (KJV)

There is nothing more unappealing to the flesh and mind than the thought of getting quiet before God. Such times are necessary, however, if we are to develop spiritually. Notice in the verse above, the connection between waiting on the Lord and spiritual strength and progress. Believers who will learn to wait before Him will find themselves able to do things that they previously could not.

MARINATING

We often eat chicken in our home, however, we rarely just cook it right out of the package. We first submit the chicken to a process called marinating. Marinating involves soaking the chicken in a combination of spices for a period of several hours. The chicken absorbs these spices, becoming much more flavorful and appetizing.

In the same way, believers are wise to spend time in the presence of God just waiting before Him. We could say we are *marinating* in His presence. As we soak up His presence, we take on His attributes. We are changed in His presence.

I often wait on God in the nighttime, when everything around me is quiet. I will get on the floor and just begin to worship Him quietly. I will recount His faithfulness, thanking Him over and over for all He has done in my life. I don't normally pray much in tongues during this time, rather, I just minister to the Lord, thanking and praising Him.

During these times of quiet worship, I am able to receive from God with greater clarity. Answers that I may need flow forth.

Direction and correction is received. I often see adjustments that need to be made and am able to make them quickly. These times work to soften me, making my heart sensitive and pure before Him. Waiting on the Lord helps develop a repentant heart.

Let's yield to God in all these areas, cultivating a tender, pliable heart before Him. As we do, we will be prepared for any way in which He desires to use us. We will be equipped for the era.

13
Responding to God

Learning to respond and flow with God in a service is a major area of training for the end-time revival. If two-thirds of the congregation won't even participate in worship, how will they flow with God when He moves in stronger ways? They won't. I am convinced that we have gone as far as we can go in the plan of God until we make some adjustments and learn to move with Him. We talk and pray about what God wants to do among us, but then act as though it were all up to Him. That's not the case. He has been endeavoring to move among us for years, but has often been kept waiting by an unresponsive Body. We must learn to recognize God's workings among us and respond accordingly, making movement along with Him.

Learning to flow with God has much to do with repentance. The person who lives a repentant life (being sensitive and responsive to God) will be aware of what God desires to do and will go along with Him. Only then will His presence manifest in the stronger ways that we desire. Only then will His glory fill the house. Only then will the miracles flow like an overwhelming river of the supernatural.

Many churches are full of everything except the Spirit of God. People show up and sit there like they have come to watch a movie. That's excusable when a person doesn't know any better, but many do know better. Even the new believer can quickly learn to flow with God if they are tender and teachable.

Our standards of worship have been too low. It's time to come up – to raise our standards – each one doing their part to cooperate with the flow of God in a service.

We will be equipped to reap the harvest only when we have learned to skillfully flow with God. This skill must be developed both individually and collectively as a body. God does not take people on to greater experiences if they are not faithful to respond to Him when He moves in more subtle ways. Our worship gatherings are training sessions for the end-time revival. If we fail our training sessions by refusing to cooperate with Him, we delay greater moves of God.

RESPONSIVENESS

Why do people often sit like the proverbial bump-on-the-log when it's time to enter in and go deeper with God? Some have been trained not to respond. Many churches have a culture of quietness that forbids any extemporaneous movement, either from the Lord or from the people. No raising of hands in worship, no *Amens* or other verbal responses to the Word, and certainly no manifestations of the Holy Spirit. Leaders in such churches think they are cultivating an atmosphere of reverence, but their refusal to move with God is really rebellion and empty religion. The people in these churches are just doing as they have been taught and don't know any better. They must be taught how to appropriately respond to God.

Other believers haven't been taught *against* responding to God, but neither have they been taught that they should. Because it's always easiest on the flesh to do nothing, they remain idle in the midst of God's movement. Their ignorance keeps them from entering in. A lack of knowledge, therefore, is another reason why people fail to respond to God in a service.

A third reason why people are not always responsive to God can be seen in the following verse:

> Be kind to one another, **tenderhearted**, forgiving one another, as God in Christ forgave you.
>
> *Ephesians 4:32*

TENDERNESS

Really? How does this verse have anything to do with responding to God in worship? This verse shows the condition of heart that the believer must maintain throughout his or her life. If the believer can forgive easily, they can flow easily. If they are tenderhearted toward others, they will be sensitive toward God. The reason many people just sit still instead of giving expression to what God is endeavoring to do is because they are not tenderhearted. They have not allowed God's love and God's Spirit to sufficiently penetrate their hearts. They are keeping themselves in a state of hardness and resistance because it's more comfortable for them to do so.

Some may protest, *That's unfair. I am sensitive and tenderhearted. I just don't have a demonstrative personality.* We're not talking about personality here. If an individual's personality is keeping them from moving with God, it means their flesh is controlling their life. Personality is not a valid excuse for disobedience. If someone is truly tenderhearted and Spirit-filled, they will learn to override their flesh and flow with God.

MY FRUSTRATION

I am sympathetic to the person who says, *I want to flow with God, but I just don't know how.* I traveled for seven years with one of the greatest ministers on earth, during a time when spiritual manifestations abounded in the Body of Christ. For about the first three or four years of my tenure, however, I failed to experience what others were experiencing in the services: the overwhelming fulness of the Spirit, the dancing, running, laughing, etc.

I was a participant to the best of my ability, but I never seemed to be able to enter in like the others. I could get in the flow and follow along, but couldn't seem to sense the promptings to which others were yielding.

Mine wasn't a case of rebellion or hardness of heart as much as it was a case of an under-developed spirit and an over-dependence on intellect. Simply put, my mind was on the throne in my life, not my spirit. (A Christian's mind is not capable of sensing spiritual movement.) Even though I was in the midst of a great outpouring, I had to make a U-turn from my years of approaching God intellectually. That took some time. I had to develop my spirit, so I could yield to God's Spirit.

We are to use our minds, of course, but we must not substitute thinking for yielding. I was an intense, intricate, over-analytical person who needed to learn to shut all that off and just enjoy God's presence. I had to learn to sense His movement, and I had to crucify my flesh in order to respond to the promptings of God. As I kept a tender heart, God graciously helped me move into His flow.

None of the movement that God requires of us is the least bit difficult. A four year old can learn to respond to God. Even if a person is like I was – slow to learn – the one with a tender heart will contribute to the flow of God instead of stifling it.

BROKENNESS

Sow for yourselves righteousness; reap steadfast love; **break up your fallow ground,** *for it is the time to seek the Lord,* **that he may come and rain** *righteousness upon you.*

Hosea 10:12

What a great picture of both repentance and revival. The prophet told the people to *break up their fallow ground* in order to receive God's rain. When the Bible speaks of ground it's often speaking of the heart of man. Farmers must plow and break up the ground of their fields before that ground is suitable for planting. Believers likewise must break up the ground of their hearts, keeping them tender and pure, ready for the rain of God's Spirit.

Notice the phrase *break up*. This is similar to the word *brokenness*. We are always to keep ourselves in a broken state. I'm not speaking of brokenness in the sense of things being a mess in our lives. We want to be broken the way a wild horse would be broken: all rebellion and stubbornness expelled. Hardness is the enemy of the Christian; tenderness is where it's at. Remain tender with God by spending much time fellowshipping with Him. A person with a repentant heart is one who has learned to keep the ground of their heart broken up, ready for anything God wants to plant, able to move any direction He wants to go.

The sacrifices of God are a broken spirit; a broken and contrite heart, O God, you will not despise.

Psalms 51:17

Let's learn to walk before God broken – tender and responsive – sensitive to His every movement. We should become proficient at recognizing Him when He whispers, not just when He shouts. Be aware of His leadings throughout the day. Listen for His still, small voice. When a body of believers comes together, having practiced these things in their daily lives, God will be able to move in greater ways, and His power will flow with greater intensity. The flow of God's power is the most prominent characteristic of revival, and the heart of repentance makes that flow possible.

14
Revival Then and Now

I enjoy reading about past revivals, knowing that God never changes and is able to do today what He did yesterday. He seeks not just to duplicate the past but to outdo Himself, working in even greater ways. Anyone who has studied true moves of God over the years will agree that repentance and brokenness are prominent characteristics of revival. We have seen how repentance can take on a variety of forms, from slight adjustments to extreme turn-arounds. The revival of the last days will feature repentance in all its forms. Altars will be filled with people dedicating their hearts to God. They will arise from those altars renewed, restored, and refreshed.

We have already spoken of the revivals of Charles G. Finney, in which the townspeople would come under such conviction, they would repent from their sin for hours, or even days. Doctors would sometimes be called to the homes, as people mistook the anguish of God's conviction upon their loved ones for some kind of physical malady. The result was multitudes of genuine conversions, not the kind of half-hearted decisions for Christ that are common in our day.

In those days, people would repent and live in sorrow until they felt they had a *breakthrough* and were converted. Although these revivals bore much fruit, we understand from the Word of God that it's not necessary to wait for some kind of *righteous feeling* before receiving Christ. Although sorrow and conviction may be present, we don't *work up* a sorrowful condition to get God in the notion of saving us. Salvation is readily available to all. Repentance should be genuine, but does not necessarily have to take days, hours, or even minutes. A true change of heart can happen instantly, and a person can be saved by simply acting on the Word of God. Whether instantaneous or gradual, repentance from sin and turning to God is a part of true revival.

Azusa

One of the most powerful revivals in modern church history was the Azusa revival of the early 1900's. This revival featured the power and glory of God manifesting in outstanding ways. Repentance of a different sort was featured here, the people continually moving and flowing with God to accomplish His purposes. (Remember, in order to flow with God, one must *make the change*, moving when He moves, changing directions as He leads.)

People in the Azusa revival would sometimes just sit quietly in the presence of God while His power moved throughout the room. Those who might have come expecting to hear preaching on such nights would have had to make a change in their heart – setting aside their expectations – in order to flow with God's purpose for that particular service. Had the people not made such adjustments, the flow would have been quenched and the manifestation of His Spirit absent.

EXPECTATIONS OR EXPECTANCY?

It's appropriate to come to a service with great expectations, but we must make sure that those expectations are more than just our own personal preferences. We should come with an expectant heart, ready to flow with God in whatever ways He might desire.

I have encountered more than a few people who have expressed disappointment in a service they had just attended, their expectations having been unmet. In many of those cases, however, the service was actually outstanding; it just took on a different form than they had anticipated. Because these people had their own idea of what the service should be like, they failed to appreciate or even recognize the great things that God did.

Attitudes similar to the one illustrated above are prevalent in our day of convenience-based Christianity and work to hold revival back. We must instead possess the flexibility of heart that embraces all the different workings of God. When each believer in the church maintains a repentant heart and makes movement along with God, the purposes of God are accomplished. We see this occurring in the book of Acts.

*When the day of Pentecost arrived, they were **all together in one place**. And suddenly there came from heaven*

*a sound like a mighty rushing wind, and it filled the en-
tire house where they were sitting.*

Acts 2:1-2

UNITY

The phrase *all together in one place* is the key to why God's
power was able flow so strongly. The word translated as *together*
is a derivative of the Greek word *homo*, meaning *the same*. People don't always show up to church with their hearts and minds
in the same place, but this sameness (also translated as *in one accord*) is a requirement if the purposes of God are to be fulfilled.
If people don't arrive to church *the same* (as is usually the case),
they must be brought into a place of sameness. This is one of the
reasons why we usually begin our services with a time of con-
gregational worship. It helps bring people into one accord. Once
the people have been brought into one accord, God's power will
flow.

As a worship service progresses, people begin to see in what
ways (if any) their hearts and minds are out of alignment with
the things of God. The tenderhearted individual will instantly
make any changes necessary to realign. This is repentance, and
it's the type of repentance in which the believer most often engages. Did the members of the early Church have to make similar adjustments? Of course. Although the Bible speaks of God's
power flowing *suddenly* on the day of Pentecost, the preparation
for that power took place over the course of several days; not

very sudden at all.

> *All of these **with their minds in full agreement** devoted themselves steadfastly to prayer, [waiting together] with the women and Mary the mother of Jesus, and with His brothers.*
>
> *Acts 1:14 (AMP)*

The followers of Jesus spent days waiting on God – seeking Him in prayer – moving into unity.

When we take time out of our life to focus on God and His things, it has a tenderizing effect on our heart. Whether the followers of Jesus in Acts realized it, they were breaking up the fallow ground of their hearts by spending time in His presence. Notice the result of this time spent together with Him: their minds were in *full agreement*. When everyone comes together as one, there is no limit to what God can accomplish – no boundaries to the scope of His revival.

Becoming of one heart and mind has often been a great challenge for the Church. Many come to church with a *do not disturb* sign symbolically placed around their neck, refusing to be moved into the things of God. When a great percentage of the congregation won't move with God, the purposes of God cannot be accomplished. I'm not trying to be negative, I'm simply stating fact. Sure, God can do some things in spite of us, but His greatest works are done with us and through us. We must come together with hearts ready for change, for there is no revival without repentance.

> Now **repent** of your sins and turn to God, so that your sins may be wiped away. **Then** times of refreshment will come from the presence of the Lord, and he will again send you Jesus, your appointed Messiah.
>
> Acts 3:19-20 (NLT)

Notice the order. First repentance, *then* revival.

The revival we desire is all about change. Entire churches need to change. The spiritual landscape of our nation needs to turn and change. How ridiculous is it for us to pray for that kind of change, yet resist it in our own personal lives? We can't say that we want society to change, if we refuse to make changes in our own hearts. People complain about the direction of our country, yet they refuse to respond to God in a worship service. They talk about wanting to see souls saved, yet they won't tithe. We can't talk about wanting God to work if He can't work through us.

If it sounds like I'm repeating certain thoughts many times over, it's because I don't want people to just have a glimpse of this truth; I want the undisputed facts of the Word forever impressed upon their hearts and minds. I want people so convinced of these things that they become fully persuaded – moved to action – crusaders for change.

KEEPING THE BALANCE

Many equate repentance with sadness, however, the repentant heart is a joyful heart. The repentant heart is sensitive toward God but resistant to offense. Truly, the most enjoyable life is the repentant life.

I do not believe that real revival is achievable without real repentance. That doesn't mean, however, that everyone has to dig up their past sins in order to be *repentant*. We must remain balanced in this area. I have been to churches where they had a repentance service. The minister was encouraging everyone to *wipe the smiles off their faces and repent.* He was basically saying that since we all sin all the time, let's identify one or two recent ones to sorrowfully bring before the Lord. Although this minister's motives may have been correct, his understanding of sin and repentance was not.

I don't sin all the time and neither should you. To teach that all believers sin daily is a religious lie. We are not to resurrect old sins. It doesn't bless the Father when we bring things before Him that Christ's blood has already cleansed. There's no greater insult to the Father than to act like His Son's blood didn't get the job done.

Repentance is required for revival, but in most cases, we're just talking about a repentant heart that is flexible and tender before Him, sensitive to His movement and quick to follow through with action. If other areas of repentance are needed, then by all means, make the change. If you need to repent to another person, go ahead and make it right. If you need to make a U-turn, admitting that you have wasted time and effort by serving your own interests, do it. Turn back, and enter into His outpouring.

15

The Baptism of Repentance

THE GREATEST REVIVAL

There can be no doubt as to which was the greatest revival in history. We have previously mentioned the Great Awakenings of the 18th and 19th centuries. Then there was the Azusa outpouring at the turn of the twentieth century, followed by the Healing Revival of the 1940's and 1950's, and the Charismatic Renewal of the 1960's and 1970's. As wonderful as these movements were, however, none compared to that which took place in just three short years under the ministry of Jesus. Jesus didn't just make it into the history books, He reset the world's calendar. His ministry is the pattern – the standard – for every revival since. How did so much happen in His ministry in such a short time? It all started with repentance.

*In those days John the Baptist came preaching in the wilderness of Judea, "**Repent**, for the kingdom of heaven is at hand." For this is he who was spoken of by the prophet Isaiah when he said, "The voice of one crying in the wilderness: 'Prepare the way of the Lord; make his paths straight.'" Now John wore a garment of camel's hair and a leather belt around his waist, and his food was locusts* *and wild honey. Then Jerusalem and all Judea and all the region about the Jordan were going out to him, and they were baptized by him in the river Jordan, confessing their sins. But when he saw many of the Pharisees and Sadducees coming to his baptism, he said to them, "You brood of vipers! Who warned you to flee from the wrath to come?* **Bear fruit in keeping with repentance.** *And do not presume to say to yourselves, 'We have Abraham as our father,' for I tell you, God is able from these stones to raise up children for Abraham. Even now the axe is laid to the root of the trees. Every tree therefore that does not bear good fruit is cut down and thrown into the fire.* **"I baptize you with water for repentance,** *but he who is coming after me is mightier than I, whose sandals I am not worthy to carry. He will baptize you with the Holy Spirit and fire. His winnowing fork is in his hand, and he will clear his threshing floor and gather his wheat into the barn, but the chaff he will burn with unquenchable fire.*

Matthew 3:1-12

This passage shows one of the reasons why Jesus was able to accomplish so much in such a short period of time. (It's not just that He was God. Jesus ministered on earth as a man anointed by the Spirit, the way anyone today would minister.) He ministered on earth so effectively because the people to whom He was ministering had been prepared ahead of time to receive.

What was it anyway that made Jesus' ministry so remarkable? We love everything about Him, of course, but I would say that the most remarkable feature of His ministry was the level of power that flowed as He ministered. Multitudes would be healed in one day. Miracles abounded. Supernatural multiplication took place. These kinds of results require a strong concentration of God's power. As we saw in the Book of Acts, for God's power to flow in such measures, a place must be prepared to receive it.

The people in Jesus' day didn't have revelation concerning how to flow with God. They weren't born again. They hadn't been taught New Testament truth. They could, however, prepare their hearts to receive. They could get in position. They could make the change. Under the ministry of John the Baptist, that's exactly what happened.

JOHN THE BAPTIST

Although John the Baptist never performed one miracle, Jesus called him one of the greatest prophets of all time (Matthew 11:11). Why? With only a message of repentance, John was able to prepare the hearts of an entire company of people. (Getting a large group of people to do anything together can be difficult; getting them all turned in a different direction, hearts open and positioned for change, is downright miraculous.) Had John not been the *Prophet of Repentance* in his day, it's doubtful that the ministry of Jesus would have taken off like it did. Yes, Jesus was anointed, but people must cooperate with God's anointing for it to flow. They must repent. They must make the change.

John the Baptist was an unusual vessel in an unusual place who was used of God in an unusual way. Everything he did went against conventional wisdom. That sounds just like God.

There are several important truths that can be seen in this passage in Matthew 3. Notice just a few of them:

> *Repent, for the kingdom of heaven is at hand.*
>
> *Matthew 3:2*

This was an interesting proclamation. John didn't say, *Repent, for the Messiah is coming,* he said, *Repent, for the kingdom of heaven is at hand.* Obviously, John's message was on target, for when Jesus came He indeed preached the *gospel of the kingdom.* The people to whom John preached were not just being prepared to meet the Messiah, they were being prepared for an entirely new way of living. Much of what they had previously known about life and God was about to change. The only way they could receive this change was to first position their hearts for change. They had to repent.

THE KINGDOM

A kingdom is a *realm* or *domain.* Different kingdoms have different laws, just as different towns may have different laws. Jesus was to introduce the world to the *kingdom of God* – a completely different way of doing things – a new realm with new laws that superseded the natural laws they had been used to. Their repentance would help align them with God's kingdom, allowing them to benefit from the laws of that kingdom. Today, these same laws benefit us, but only to the degree that we maintain our alignment with them. When we go against God's laws, they begin to work against us instead of working for us.

Repentance in preparation for the kingdom meant more than just turning from sin, although that was included. They were consecrating themselves to a system of living that was largely unfamiliar. No one yet knew about *who we are in Christ.* They didn't yet know about the love of God that would replace the ten commandments. All they knew was that change was coming across-the-board. Their repentance was a heart-consecration to change. Anything and everything was on the table. This baptism of repentance – preparation for the ministry of Jesus – was an amazing move of God in its own right.

BAPTISM

They were baptized by him in the river Jordan, confessing their sins.

Matthew 3:6

Baptism was a most appropriate action for the type of change that was about to take place in these people. The Jews of the day understood the essence of baptism, a form of it having been part of the Levitical laws of cleansing. The idea is, you go down one way and come up another way. Baptism is all about change.

Baptism took repentance a step further: demonstrating outwardly what was taking place inwardly. The valuable lesson here: if what's in your heart is real, it will affect your actions, changing what you think, say, and do.

If repentance *can* include action, it *should* include it. These people were doing whatever they could. They could not yet have a recreated heart but they could still have a repentant heart. They couldn't yet receive the remission of sins, but they could position themselves for forgiveness of sins. They could make movement away from sin and toward God, pointing themselves in the right direction. They were in receiving-mode, ready for change.

As for myself, I indeed immerse you in water because of repentance. But He who is coming after me is mightier than I, whose sandals I am not worthy to carry. He himself will baptize you in the sphere of and by means of the Holy Spirit and fire.

Matthew 3:11 (WST)

Had they failed to make the heart-change necessary for water baptism, they would have not been in position to receive later, when it came time for Spirit baptism. What John introduced with his baptism meant massive change. (That's one reason why they were out in the wilderness instead of back in town. It's sometimes necessary to leave that which is familiar and natural, and instead journey out into neutral territory.) What Jesus would later bring to the people was a level of change that was every bit as dramatic as John's baptism.

STRAIGHT PATHS

John's emphasis on repentance was something that didn't make sense to me for many years, but I now see with greater clarity. He was indeed preparing a way for the Lord, *making His paths straight* (Matthew 3:3). This verse from Luke sheds more light on what that means:

> *Every valley shall be filled, and every mountain and hill shall be made low, and the crooked shall become straight, and the rough places shall become level ways, and all flesh shall see the salvation of God.*
>
> *Luke 3:5-6*

When a person has only a limited amount of time (as was the case with the ministry of Jesus), a direct route on the interstate is much quicker than winding mountain roads. God wants us able to easily receive that which He has for us. What are the valleys, mountains, crooked roads, and rough places being spoken of in this passage? They are symbolic of the different conditions of man's heart. A repentant heart does away with the valleys of low, unworthy thinking, the high mountains of prideful thinking, the crooked places of the wounds and complications of life, and the bumpy paths of being out of the will of God. The repentant heart is one that's ready to directly receive the salvation of God. God's power is free to come right in and do its liberating work. Thank God for repentance.

REPENTANCE AND REVELATION

> *I myself did not know him, but for this purpose I came baptizing with water,* **that he might be revealed** *to Israel.*
>
> *John 1:31*

John came preaching change so that Christ might be revealed to the world. No change, no revelation. Without the baptism of repentance, the people would likely not even have recognized Jesus as Messiah. Jesus had to be revealed to the people of His day, just as He must be revealed to people today.

The revelation of truth to a person's spirit is a supernatural happening. (No human can impart revelation to another human unless God is at work.) A revelation requires a reception: a receiving heart. There is no receiving heart where there is no repentant heart. How important was John's ministry? Without John's ministry of repentance, Jesus might not even have had a ministry of power. It's becoming clear to us why Jesus spoke of John as being so great.

I understand that statements connecting the effectiveness of

Jesus' ministry to anything or anyone else are distasteful to the religious mind, but it's the clear teaching of the Word of God. Notice this example, where the people sitting under Jesus' ministry had obviously never sat under John's:

> *Is not this the carpenter, the son of Mary and brother of James and Joses and Judas and Simon? And are not his sisters here with us?" And **they took offense at him**. And Jesus said to them, "A prophet is not without honor, except in his hometown and among his relatives and in his own household." And **he could do no mighty work there**, except that he laid his hands on a few sick people and healed them. And he marveled because of their unbelief. And he went about among the villages teaching.*
>
> *Mark 6:3-6*

Jesus did no mighty work in His hometown because His ministry was not received there. They didn't receive because they couldn't make the change from carpenter to prophet. They continued to see Jesus as they had known Him His whole life because their hearts had not been prepared for change. There was no repentance, therefore there was no revival: no receiving, no responding, no refreshing. How significant this is. In the midst of the greatest revival the world has ever known, we see an entire town excluded. Not because God didn't desire to work, but because they refused to make the change.

Notice, however, the last phrase of this passage: *he went about among the villages teaching.* Jesus didn't just give up on these people, but He did have to back up, taking time to teach the first principles that they had managed to miss. Teaching the Word enlightens people, helping them to recognize their hour of visitation. Jesus' teaching tour through Nazareth was an example of *God's kindness. . . . meant to lead you to repentance* (Romans 2:4).

JESUS' BAPTISM

Let's speak further about Jesus' ministry. Before He stepped into His public ministry, He stepped into the waters of Jordan to be baptized by John. Did Jesus, the Son of God, really need to repent? Yes and no. Jesus was sinless, therefore He did not have to repent for sin (as a sinner would). He was, however, specifically led to participate in John's baptism: the baptism of repentance.

> *Then Jesus came from Galilee to the Jordan to John, to be baptized by him. John would have prevented him, saying, "I need to be baptized by you, and do you come to me?" But Jesus answered him, "Let it be so now, for thus it is fitting for us to fulfill all righteousness." Then he consented.*
>
> *Matthew 3:13-15*

John was initially not on board with Jesus' request to be baptized. The Amplified Bible says that John *protested strenuously.*

After all, this was the *baptism of repentance for the forgiveness of sins*. If the Messiah was coming to deal with His own sin, we would have major problems. (A sinner couldn't become the *Lamb of God that takes away the sin of the world*.) We know Jesus wasn't there for sin. On the other hand, Jesus wouldn't have cheapened John's baptism by participating for no reason. There must have been an important reason for Him to have gone down into the water.

Remember, repentance, although often associated with sin, is not exclusively connected with sin. As we have learned, repentance is a change of heart and renewal of mind. Repentance is all about change.

Did Jesus need to change? Absolutely. Although He wasn't off course in life, He was in transition. He needed to bring a heart of change before His Father, submitting to His will. He was about to experience the biggest change in His life so far, as He stepped into the ministry that God had for Him.

Jesus wasn't all-knowing as He walked the earth, but neither was He in the dark. He had at least some revelation of what the next three years might be like. He had read the Scriptures. He knew that the Messiah would suffer. Much of what lay before Him was not easy. Even His miracle ministry would not be easy on His flesh. Change (especially change that involves the unknown) is uncomfortable for anyone, including Jesus.

The purpose of Jesus' baptism was for Him to make a public commitment of His private consecration: to make the dramatic change that lay before Him and step into His ministry. What do we call it when someone turns from the desires of flesh and self, and commits to God? Repentance. Jesus went down one way (as a carpenter), and came up another way (as a minister). He made the change.

One needs only to look at the Father's response to Jesus' baptism to see how significant this act of obedience was.

> *And when Jesus was baptized, immediately he went up from the water, and behold, the heavens were opened to him, and he saw the Spirit of God descending like a dove and coming to rest on him; and behold, a voice from heaven said, "This is my beloved Son, with whom I am well pleased."*
>
> *Matthew 3:16-17*

Jesus made the change. He made the commitment to align himself with the purposes of God. What was the result? A continuous flow from heaven. Heaven opened, power was released, and the voice of God manifested. In the same way, when God sees a repentant heart in us, the Spirit can fall, power can flow freely, and we can clearly hear from Him.

What if Jesus hadn't submitted His heart, soul, and body to that baptism? He wouldn't have possessed the level of commitment necessary to walk out the will of God. He wouldn't have stepped into the fullness of His ministry. He wouldn't have, at the same time, received the empowerment of the Holy Spirit. Because He submitted to the waters of repentance, He was able a short time later to turn water into wine. His consecrated heart allowed the greatest revival in history to commence.

Thank God for Jesus' example of consecration and change. Thank God for repentance.

16
People Who Repented
(and Others Who Should Have)

Repenting and receiving are connected. This is not because God likes to see us when we're down; God likes to see us receive. Remember, one of the main instances of repentance occurs as the believer responds and moves along with God. The connection between repenting and receiving is a matter of spiritual law. If a person won't repent, even God cannot help them.

> *He who is often reproved, yet stiffens his neck, will suddenly be broken beyond healing.*
>
> *Proverbs 29:1*

Stubbornness, hard-headedness, and rebellion guarantee destruction in a person's life. On the other hand, being teachable, even when uncomfortable, can guarantee success in life.

Repentance is a prominent theme throughout Scripture. When we see repentance on display, things go well with people, even if some of the consequences of their actions are irreversible. When people fail to repent, however, things do not go well. Even though someone may be a good person, failure to come before God – to make the change and make things right – keeps good things at bay.

All have sinned (including you and me), so we all understand the need for repentance. Because we've all missed it, we should refrain from looking down our noses in judgement when others miss it. We are not to be occupied with the sins of others, rather, we are to be occupied with the grace of God that keeps us day-to-day. Although our focus is not on sin, it is still beneficial to look at the lives of some of the people in the Bible who missed it. We can identify why they missed it, look for repentance, and note the results.

ADAM

And they heard the sound of the Lord God walking in the garden in the cool of the day, and the man and his wife hid themselves from the presence of the Lord God among the trees of the garden. But the Lord God called to the man and said to him, "Where are you?" And he said, "I heard the sound of you in the garden, and I was afraid, because I was naked, and I hid myself." He said, "Who told you that you were naked? Have you eaten of the tree of which I commanded you not to eat?" The man said, "The woman whom you gave to be with me, she gave me fruit of the tree, and I ate." Then the Lord God said to the woman, "What is this that you have done?" The woman said, "The serpent deceived me, and I ate."

Genesis 3:8-13

It's not necessary to hear a sermon or read a book on repentance to know that you need to do it. If a child is brought up correctly, they know to say *sorry* when they find themselves in hot water. When a person knows God intimately, they know that repentance is sometimes a necessary course of action. The first man, Adam, knew God intimately.

I find it interesting that the Scriptures show no hint of repentance on the part of Adam or his wife, Eve. This is the passage of Scripture that first mentions sin. When the Bible mentions anything for the first time it sets precedent and is worthy of extra attention. For repentance to be absent here is particularly significant.

We see blame-shifting, excuses, and denial, but no heart-change. The results? We barely hear of Adam again. Although he lived for centuries after his sin, there was nothing remarkable enough about his life to warrant further mention in the Scriptures.

This was a man who had experience with God that no one else on earth had. Because of how rapidly sin progressed on the earth, it's reasonable to believe that Adam did very little to spread his knowledge of God to others. Although full restoration may not have been possible for Adam, repentance was still in order. Instead of opening his heart to express sorrow, Adam seems to have just shut down where his relationship with God was concerned. Let's not follow his example.

SAUL

*And Samuel said, "Though you are little in your own
eyes, are you not the head of the tribes of Israel? The
Lord anointed you king over Israel. And the Lord sent
you on a mission and said, 'Go, devote to destruction
the sinners, the Amalekites, and fight against them until
they are consumed.' Why then did you not obey the voice
of the Lord? Why did you pounce on the spoil and do
what was evil in the sight of the Lord?" And Saul said
to Samuel, "I have obeyed the voice of the Lord. I have
gone on the mission on which the Lord sent me. I have
brought Agag the king of Amalek, and I have devoted
the Amalekites to destruction. But the people took of
the spoil, sheep and oxen, the best of the things devoted
to destruction, to sacrifice to the Lord your God in Gil-
gal." And Samuel said, "Has the Lord as great delight in
burnt offerings and sacrifices, as in obeying the voice of
the Lord? Behold, to obey is better than sacrifice, and to
listen than the fat of rams. For rebellion is as the sin of
divination, and presumption is as iniquity and idolatry.
Because you have rejected the word of the Lord, he has
also rejected you from being king." Saul said to Samuel, "I
have sinned, for I have transgressed the commandment
of the Lord and your words, because I feared the people*

and obeyed their voice. Now therefore, please pardon my
sin and return with me that I may bow before the Lord."
And Samuel said to Saul, "I will not return with you.
For you have rejected the word of the Lord, and the Lord
has rejected you from being king over Israel."

1 Samuel 15:22-26

King Saul was quite a character. After denying his sin, then blaming the people for his sin, this passage appears to show Saul's heartfelt repentance. This was not true repentance, however; it was false. False repentance looks and sounds just like the real thing, but there is no heart-change. How do we know that Saul's repentance was false? It was not received by the Prophet Samuel, who was there on behalf of God. If God doesn't receive your repentance, you didn't repent. You may have cried, but you didn't change.

Saul initially argued with Samuel, only expressing regret once he saw that his excuses wouldn't work and Samuel had him backed into a corner. To *regret* is not the same thing as to *repent*. Regret is sorrow without change. Saul never made the change. He didn't repent, therefore he was not able to receive and be restored.

We read this verse previously:

Bear fruit in keeping with repentance.

Matthew 3:8

If repentance is real, change will manifest in every area. Saul went right back to his own way of doing things, rather than submitting to authority. There was no fruit because there was no real repentance. He thought his position as king excused him from aligning with God, however, God gives no one a free pass for sin. God disregards insincerity today, just as He did in King Saul's day. This is a valuable lesson for us.

What if Saul had been genuine? What if his repentance had been real, and his greatest concern at the moment was not how to save face as a leader, but how he had allowed himself to be deceived in the first place? He might have left a legacy instead of leaving a mess. Unfortunately, he never softened his heart. Because he never made the change, his destiny changed. This king, who had showed so much promise, went forward without God's anointing from this moment on.

DAVID

The accounts recorded in 2 Samuel 11-12 are among the most sobering pages in the Bible. They recount King David's affair with Bathsheba and the subsequent murder of her husband, Uriah. I recommend taking time right now to read these two chapters, as space constraints make reprinting them here impractical.

This story is as scandalous as anything recorded in Scripture. I swallow hard as I read it, because the perpetrator, David, was known as a man after God's own heart. He indeed was a man with a heart for God, yet he still yielded to sin. How did this happen? David let his guard down. He allowed himself to become spiritually weak, even as his kingdom was peaking in strength. This same thing could happen to any of us, should we allow our lives to be dominated by our flesh.

It's obvious that the once-tenderhearted David was not his usual self, because he did not initiate repentance on his own. He hardened himself in order to continue down the road he was on. Even so, God's great love still reached out to him. The following is the rebuke that was delivered to David by the Prophet Nathan:

> *Why have you despised the word of the Lord, to do what is evil in his sight? You have struck down Uriah the Hittite with the sword and have taken his wife to be your wife and have killed him with the sword of the Ammonites. Now therefore the sword shall never depart from your house, because you have despised me and have taken the wife of Uriah the Hittite to be your wife. Thus says the Lord, 'Behold, I will raise up evil against you out of your own house. And I will take your wives before your eyes and give them to your neighbor, and he shall lie with your wives in the sight of this sun. For you did it secretly, but I will do this thing before all Israel and before the sun. David said to Nathan, "**I have sinned against the Lord.**" And Nathan said to David, "The Lord also has put away your sin; you shall not die. Nevertheless,*

because by this deed you have utterly scorned the Lord, the child who is born to you shall die." Then Nathan went to his house.

2 *Samuel 12:9-12*

David's response to Nathan wasn't long, but his heart of repentance was one hundred percent real. There were stiff consequences that David could not change. This was going to cost him. It stung David deeply, yet it was nothing compared to the way he had violated Uriah and Bathsheba. When the child Bathsheba bore to David grew sick and was at the point of death, David lay before the Lord in repentance. He had been told the situation wouldn't change but David leaned hard on the mercy of the Lord anyway. That honors God. Repentance honors God.

David's repentant heart allowed him to recover from a situation from which very few people can recover. He made the change, and God was able to restore.

David's quick response sounded very similar to Saul's response. David's, however, was real repentance while Saul's was not. Remember, God sees the heart. When words proceed from our mouths, God can tell whether they originate from the heart. This was an instance of major repentance. David didn't just respond to Nathan, he also poured his heart out before God.

Create in me a clean heart, O God, and renew a right spirit within me. Cast me not away from your presence, and take not your Holy Spirit from me. Restore to me the joy of your salvation, and uphold me with a willing spirit.

Psalms 51:10-12

David realized that he had allowed himself to be deceived. He believed the lie that somehow his actions were justifiable. When he came to himself and repented, he identified the fact that he had walked away from the truth.

Behold, you delight in truth in the inward being. . . .

Psalms 51:6

DAVID AND BATHSHEBA

We have seen David's repentance both before Nathan and before the Lord, but how did he handle things with Bathsheba? Did he repent to her? Bathsheba, through no fault of her own, endured a season of unthinkable hardship. Being home alone while your husband is off at war would in itself qualify as a time of great difficulty. That, however, was the easy part of her year.

When Bathsheba received a knock at her door telling her to fix herself up for a meeting with the king, thoughts must have come at her from every direction. *What could the king want with me? Did something happen to Uriah?* David knew Uriah well. He was one of the mighty men of valor who helped bring him to power. Now, Uriah's wife is standing in his bedchamber. Bathsheba, shocked at what David has in mind, is forced to stare betrayal in the face, and then bare all to please the king. Whatever they called this in David's day, we would call it rape.

A short time later, Bathsheba discovers that not only was she violated, she is pregnant. Her secret shame is about to turn into public humiliation. Everyone knew that Uriah had been away for an extended period of time. What would she tell people? How could she tell her sweetheart when he came back from war? David solved that problem. Uriah didn't come back from war.

The death of her husband was almost more than she could bear. 2 Samuel 11:26 says that Bathsheba *lamented* for Uriah. The Hebrew word translated as *lamented* means *to grieve violently.* When she needed him the most, the man that she loved was ripped away from her. Uriah's death broke Bathsheba's heart. Perhaps she blamed herself for not being stronger before David. Maybe she thought that somehow her unfaithfulness caused her husband to be killed.

Although no one should have to endure all that she did, more sorrow was just ahead. The child that Bathsheba bore to David died. We are not told the age of this child, but the death of a child at any age is traumatic for a parent. This was surely not the life she had imagined.

Living in David's kingdom, Bathsheba knew all about God: the stories, the miracles, the testimonies of deliverance, the heroes of faith. As the victim of David's hypocrisy, however, it would have been natural for her to have become bitter, feeling as though God had forsaken and forgotten her.

Then this happens:

> *Then David comforted his wife, Bathsheba, and went in*
> *to her and lay with her, and she bore a son, and he called*
> *his name Solomon. And the Lord loved him.*
>
> 2 Samuel 12:24

This verse doesn't seem all that remarkable on the surface, but it's actually the turning point in this story. The events of this verse affected the entire kingdom of Israel. What was it that was so significant?

David comforted his wife.

This doesn't mean he just put his arm around her and said, *Cheer up. Things will get better.* He wasn't tossing around comforting phrases, trying to get her in bed again. For Bathsheba to have been able to receive comfort from anyone, least-of-all David, is astounding. She was what some would call *damaged goods*, however, this verse appears to indicate a change within her.

The word translated here as *comforted* is the Hebrew word *naham*. Although it does indeed often mean *comfort*, it is also frequently translated as *repent*. With this in mind, let's look again at the first phrase of this verse:

Then David repented to his wife, Bathsheba.

Something tremendously deep and beautiful took place here. Having made the change before God, David now approaches Bathsheba to make things right. The vain, selfish, slick-talking personality that had seduced her was gone: empty and broken. David humbles himself before her, expressing heartfelt sorrow, holding nothing back. He repents.

She might not have known it before, but now Bathsheba knows that Uriah wasn't randomly killed in battle. David had ordered the hit.

Did he really tell her that? It wouldn't have been full repentance had he left out such a major detail. David came clean. He came to her with the *clean heart* and *right spirit* that the Lord had created within him. He broke down before her with all sincerity. When he took her hand, looked her in the eyes, and through tears said, *I am so sorry,* something powerful happened. God was able to inhabit David's words. Divine love penetrated Bathsheba's heart, working in her a much-needed healing and restoration. The pain that would have likely lingered throughout her lifetime was replaced by God's love. How powerful repentance is.

David did indeed lay with Bathsheba again, but this time it was different. It wasn't forced, it was a flow. It wasn't just sexual, it was also spiritual: intimate and God-filled. Out of this encounter came Solomon: the wisest, wealthiest, and most powerful of all the kings of the earth. Repentance brought him forth. Repentance gave birth to wisdom, riches, and power. It will do the same today.

Most people haven't treated their spouse (or others) the way

David treated Bathsheba. I understand that. But many, nonetheless, have violated those with whom they were in covenant.
Some have cheated. Some have lied. Some have chosen to just ignore those with whom they were once in love. Regardless of the
offense, all can follow David's example of repentance and enjoy
the results that follow. Couples, ready to divorce, can have a new
marriage in ten minutes if they would only repent. Repentance
works miracles. Repentance, when genuine, changes everything.
I love the power of repentance.

ASA

There were good kings and bad kings in Israel and Judah's
history. Asa was one of the good ones. The rise of his kingdom
shows one good decision after another, his country prospering
as a result. Asa missed it, however, by forgetting who had giv-
en him his great success. This error is one that all must guard
against. We must not seek God while desperate for victory, only
to abandon Him once we have the victory. Notice the Lord's rebuke to Asa, and Asa's response:

*At that time Hanani the seer came to Asa king of Judah
and said to him, "Because you relied on the king of Syria, and did not rely on the Lord your God, the army of
the king of Syria has escaped you. Were not the Ethiopi-
ans and the Libyans a huge army with very many char-*

*iots and horsemen? Yet because you relied on the Lord,
he gave them into your hand. For the eyes of the Lord
run to and fro throughout the whole earth, to give strong
support to those whose heart is blameless toward him.
You have done foolishly in this, for from now on you will
have wars." Then Asa was angry with the seer and put
him in the stocks in prison, for he was in a rage with him
because of this. And Asa inflicted cruelties upon some of
the people at the same time. The acts of Asa, from first
to last, are written in the Book of the Kings of Judah and
Israel. In the thirty-ninth year of his reign Asa was dis-
eased in his feet, and his disease became severe. Yet even
in his disease he did not seek the Lord, but sought help
from physicians. And Asa slept with his fathers, dying in
the forty-first year of his reign.*

2 Chronicles 16:7-13

Are you kidding me? After a lifetime seeking and serving
God, Asa let one correction permanently sidetrack him. God
sent a prophet to him, just as He had with David, but Asa's response was nothing like David's. Asa took offense at the prophet's rebuke and threw him in jail. (Here's a lesson for all of us: if
a correction enrages you, *you* are the one who is missing it, not
the person bringing the correction.) We are always to remain
teachable and correctable. This wasn't just one of the citizens of
the kingdom bringing the correction, it was God's prophet. The
king was to be a partaker of the prophet's ministry. This time,

however, Asa would have none of it.

Not only did Asa stop relying on the Lord, he began yielding to the devil, cruelly oppressing his own people. When we harden our heart to little things (like correction) it will eventually lead to bigger problems. When disease showed up in the king's life, there was no repentance to be found. Asa was in the flow of hardness instead of the flow of repentance. It wasn't the disease in Asa's feet that cost him his life, it was the hardness in his heart. That hardness began years earlier when he wouldn't listen to the prophet. Let's listen and live. Let's be people who will receive correction and instruction. Let's keep a repentant heart and be quick to make the change.

HEZEKIAH

Hezekiah was another good king; a really good one, in fact. He made some missteps here and there, even toward the end of his life, but by-and-large he did well. One of the reasons for his success was his relationship with the Prophet Isaiah. Another reason for his success? A repentant heart.

> *In those days Hezekiah became sick and was at the point of death. And Isaiah the prophet the son of Amoz came to him, and said to him, "Thus says the Lord: Set your house in order, for you shall die, you shall not recover."* **Then Hezekiah turned** *his face to the wall and prayed*

*to the Lord, and said, "Please, O Lord, remember how I have walked before you in faithfulness and with a whole heart, and have done what is good in your sight." **And Hezekiah wept bitterly.** Then the word of the Lord came to Isaiah: "Go and say to Hezekiah, Thus says the Lord, the God of David your father: I have heard your prayer; I have seen your tears. Behold, I will add fifteen years to your life. I will deliver you and this city out of the hand of the king of Assyria, and will defend this city.*

Isaiah 38:1-6

Hezekiah turned to God, making an instant, genuine heart-change. We're not told that there was any sin to repent of, per se. It's not always the case that there is some major sin. Repent anyway. If the Lord says you're going to die, don't just die. Repent. Get on your face and talk to the Lord about it like Hezekiah did. Isaiah had barely left the palace when the Lord sent him back with a much improved report. Because Hezekiah repented and made the change, God was able to repent and make the change. Hezekiah's repentance bought him fifteen more years of life. What if he hadn't repented? He would have died early.

UZZIAH

He set himself to seek God in the days of Zechariah,

> *who instructed him in the fear of God, and as long as he*
> *sought the Lord, God made him prosper.*
>
> 2 Chronicles 26:5

This verse is speaking about King Uzziah, another one of Israel's good kings. He hungered and sought after God, maintaining an open and teachable heart. The Prophet Zechariah (a different Zechariah than the author of the book of Zechariah) was able to regularly impart truth into his life. As a result, both Uzziah and his kingdom prospered. As was the case with others, however, Uzziah made the mistake of trusting in his prosperity, forgetting how he got there.

> *But when he was strong, **he grew proud, to his destruction**. For he was unfaithful to the Lord his God and entered the temple of the Lord to burn incense on the altar of incense. But Azariah the priest went in after him, with eighty priests of the Lord who were men of valor, and they withstood King Uzziah and said to him, "It is not for you, Uzziah, to burn incense to the Lord, but for the priests, the sons of Aaron, who are consecrated to burn incense. Go out of the sanctuary, for you have done wrong, and it will bring you no honor from the Lord God." Then Uzziah was angry. Now he had a censer in his hand to burn incense, and when he became angry with the priests, leprosy broke out on his forehead in the*

presence of the priests in the house of the Lord, by the altar of incense. And Azariah the chief priest and all the priests looked at him, and behold, he was leprous in his forehead! And they rushed him out quickly, and he himself hurried to go out, because the Lord had struck him. And King Uzziah was a leper to the day of his death, and being a leper lived in a separate house, for he was excluded from the house of the Lord. And Jotham his son was over the king's household, governing the people of the land.

2 Chronicles 26:16-21

Again, we see no mention of repentance, nor fruits of repentance. Uzziah could have been set free from his disease at any time, had he repented. He instead maintained his arrogance – his stiff-necked *you can't teach me anything* attitude – and enjoyed a life of seclusion with only his leprosy to keep him company. It's amazing what people will choose in place of repentance. Repentance or leprosy? I'd choose repentance. Uzziah should have repented.

It's interesting to observe who is missing from the above passage. We see no further mention of Zechariah, the prophet who discipled Uzziah in the things of God. It's very likely that, somewhere along the way, Uzziah left Zechariah, his spiritual father. (Even if Zechariah had died, Uzziah should have continued to follow his teaching.) When we leave the person to whom God has connected us, we open ourselves up to deception and destruction. Just because a person moves into a higher position, or goes out on their own, doesn't release them from the influence of the leaders who raised them in the things of God. Stay with those to whom God has connected you, and stay safe.

PAUL

As I was on my way and drew near to Damascus, about noon a great light from heaven suddenly shone around me. And I fell to the ground and heard a voice saying to me, 'Saul, Saul, why are you persecuting me?' And I answered, 'Who are you, Lord?' And he said to me, 'I am Jesus of Nazareth, whom you are persecuting.' Now those who were with me saw the light but did not understand the voice of the one who was speaking to me. And I said, 'What shall I do, Lord?' And the Lord said to me, 'Rise, and go into Damascus, and there you will be told all that is appointed for you to do.'

Acts 22:6-10

We spoke earlier of adjustments, course corrections, and U-turns. It's safe to say that, on this day on the Damascus road, one of the biggest U-turns in history took place. What's even more amazing is how quickly it happened. When Paul found out he had been going the wrong direction, he instantly made the change. Yes, Paul's ministry was legendary, his writings timeless, and his teaching revelatory, but behind all that was a heart that went from resisting to submitting in a moment. I'm struck by how fast he was able to repent. Paul's heart of repentance was inspiring and amazing, like nothing I've ever seen.

There he was on the road to Damascus. He had all the necessary papers. This was going to be his biggest bust yet. He could visualize the cart full of Christians being trucked away to prison. He was about to purge Damascus of the cancerous stench of Christianity when, within just a few minutes, he was born again. That's quite a turn-around. He asked the Lord, *Who are you?* and *What do I do?* Those were his only questions. No arguments. No excuses. No deflecting blame. Talk about making the change. Paul wins the award for the most dramatic change in the shortest amount of time.

Why was Paul able to be used so greatly? Was it his education? His leadership abilities? His charismatic personality or rugged good looks? None of that. It was his heart. Do you want to be used like Paul, David, or Jesus? You can. It just takes a repentant heart. A heart that is open, submissive, and responsive before God. A heart that will (say it with me) *make the change.*

17
Full Steam Ahead

People get ready, there's a train a comin'
You don't need no baggage, you just get on board
All you need is faith, to hear the diesels hummin'
Don't need no ticket, you just thank the Lord

The lyrics above are from a gospel-inspired pop song called *People Get Ready*, one of the top 25 songs of all time. I quote these lyrics because the first line gives us a picture of what needs to happen right now in the Body of Christ.

If we as the Church don't get ready and *make the change*, we will miss the train of revival. This train is about to speed up and gain some serious momentum, and I plan to be on board. There are others – churches, ministers, believers – that are in danger of not being on board. My suggestion: get on board. My second suggestion: if you're not on board, get out of the way before you get run over.

It's time to really mean that we want revival, or stop talking about it. If we want it, let's act like it. Let's not quench it when it comes. The Church should never be guilty of lip service: talking a good talk, but having our hearts far away. We are not to be hypocrites: saying one thing but doing another. We have been sternly warned not to allow ourselves to become lukewarm.

I often minister in churches. It's my job. Although I don't know everything and am always learning, I have noticed some patterns in many of our services. Often, as we are gathered together, the Spirit falls. Times of refreshing come. The glory fills the room. The stage is set to go higher, but we never seem to go higher. We quit. We say, *It's time to go* after only 30 minutes. Sometimes the move is shut down by the people. Sometimes it's shut down by the one who is most vocal about wanting revival: the pastor.

A Plea to Pastors

One of my spiritual mentors spoke of a time when he was ministering at a large church. The power of God was present to minister to the people in an unusual way. However, just as this minister was about to step out and deliver that power to the people, the pastor walked up behind him and said, *You're done.* What do you do when that happens? Nothing. You're done. Go sit down.

A while back, I had a similar experience while ministering at a church. The pastor was out of the country and had asked me to speak on the same subject upon which he had been ministering: the gifts of the Spirit. That was no problem for me; it's a subject with which I'm very comfortable. (When I am ministering for a pastor who is away, I exercise an abundance of caution to follow any instructions I am given. I would never want a pastor to trust me with his congregation only to come home to a mess.)

As I began ministering, I could sense that very few of these people were filled with the Spirit. (You can preach all day long on the gifts of the Spirit, but if a person is not filled with the Spirit they will never be used to minister the gifts.) I stayed with my assignment, but began to interject more thoughts regarding the necessity of the Baptism of the Holy Spirit. As I wound down my message, I invited people who wanted to receive this baptism – the infilling of the Spirit – to come forward. Only a few came, even though at least a few dozen should have come.

As the people came forward, I was shocked at who else came forward: the associate pastor. He stepped in front of me and took the service over. I was just getting ready to pray with these people to be filled when he took the mic away. (By the way, this was a full gospel church that was supposed to have believed in this experience.)

The associate pastor began to speak, *Now I think what we all need to do, rather than hastily jumping into anything, is just go home and reflect on what Joel said here this morning.* Reflect? That's just an excuse for not acting on the Word. We need more action and less reflection. *Hastily jumping in* is exactly what needed to happen that morning.

This associate pastor shut me down, so I went and sat down. He didn't want full people in the church because he likely wasn't filled with the Spirit himself. He was filled with religion and intellectualism. I could have cried. Not because he took over the service; I don't care about that. I was weeping on the inside because I could see hunger on the faces of some of these people, and their leader refused to allow that hunger to be satisfied. I left that church wondering why I even came.

I can say with authority that the Lord won't put up with such hypocrisy. If that church and others like it fail to repent and make the change, they will cease to exist and God will raise up others. Let's repent instead of being removed. If you or your church has held back revival, get on your face and repent before the Lord. Let the tears be genuine and the repentance real. (If a church doesn't know any better, that's different, but this was a church that had been teaching on the gifts of the Spirit. They did know better.)

Do we want this revival or not? If so, then we must stop acting like we're just putting up with the move of the Spirit. Enough with the attitude that says, *We're okay with a little of this, but not too much.* Why don't we want too much? How will we ever get to the next level if we reject the fullness of the present level? You don't learn to dive or even swim by sitting in the kiddie pool talking about how excited you are for more. You must get in and continue to go deeper. The Church must keep moving with God, letting the waters of revival rise until we're in the deep places of the Spirit.

(I understand that God has a plan for every service. I also understand that not every service is supposed to feature wild manifestations and demonstrations. However, as we move further into revival, there will be a marked increase in the manifestations of God in our services.)

Pastors sometimes shut down the flow of God because they are fearful of losing control in their church, or losing people in their church. I pastored for more than a decade, so I am familiar with these issues. I understand that people can get in the flesh, act out when it's not the proper time, and try to take over. This is nothing to worry about. God and the pastor are bigger than someone's flesh. People can be taught to respond appropriately.

Will someone leave the church if real revival breaks out? Many people will leave when God's power manifests. Many others will come. I know some pastors who think that they cannot afford to have any more empty seats, but that's wrong thinking. We can't afford to be without the flow of God's power. God loves the people who are present even more than the pastor loves them. If He chooses to move anyhow, we are obligated to move with Him without considering who might be offended. Let's just obey and leave the results with God.

If God's power continues to flow, and momentum is building in a service, let's not kill it. Let's go with it. What's wrong with saying, *Hey, I know this wasn't on the schedule, but let's come back again tomorrow, and let's stay open after that to see what God will do?* There is not a major revival in history that was scheduled ahead of time. The revival of the last days will be no different. We will have to demonstrate flexibility, flowing with God.

Well, we'll wear out the children's workers if we go on. Bring the kids into the service. The glory will keep them quiet. Yes, we might wear out the workers if we try to manufacture a revival in the flesh, but it will work if God's in it. Can you imagine if everything stopped in the upper room of Acts 2 because they didn't have enough workers for the spontaneous second service that took place out in the streets? I understand that our ministries must be organized, and we should have a plan, but let's also be quick to abandon it – making the change – if that's what's called for.

Some pastors are uncomfortable with the move of God because they themselves aren't sure what to do with it. That's understandable, but it's not an excuse to forbid it. Bring in someone who does know the flow of the Spirit and everyone can learn together. Doing nothing is not an option if you want to be on the revival train. Pretending that God doesn't move that way anymore is not the answer. Deceiving yourself into thinking that there's no value in all those silly manifestations is not the way to go. There's no deeper flow without going through the flow that crucifies the flesh. We don't get to pick-and-choose with God. We need it all. Don't like it? Don't agree? That's fine, but get out of the way because this train is coming through.

It's time that nothing be off-limits to God. It's time for pastors and leaders to put their money where their mouth is and allow the power that they say they're hungry for to flow. Don't be like the churches during the great healing revival. Do you know what happened to them? They were left out. They sat on the sidelines criticizing all the evangelists while God's power flowed in tents, fields, and parking lots. Many of those churches no longer exist. Their candlestick was removed because they refused to repent, put aside their petty differences, and love people enough to not withhold God's power from them. They needed to turn back, repent, and do the *first works*.

COMMITMENT

I'm all in. I'm going all the way. I refuse to compromise just to stay comfortable. I'll make whatever changes are necessary to succeed. I don't care what others think, I just care about seeing the power of God flow, the harvest reaped, and the plan of God move forward.

Let's do whatever it takes to get this job done. Full repentance, full revival, forward energy.

Let's make the change.

Salvation

The most important decision you can make in life is the decision to receive Jesus Christ as your personal Lord and Savior. It is a decision to turn from sin and self, and to follow God, every day and in every way.

This decision to receive Christ is what the Bible calls being *born-again*, or being *saved*. Without this salvation experience, people are doomed to failure in life and eternity in hell. Success and eternal life belong to the believer in Christ. If you have been reading this book and don't know that you have been born-again, it's time to make the decision to follow Christ.

Read what God says in His word about this great experience:

Truly, truly, I say to you, whoever hears my word and believes him who sent me has eternal life. He does not come into judgment, but has passed from death to life.

John 5:24

For God so loved the world, that he gave his only Son, that whoever believes in him should not perish but have eternal life. For God did not send his Son into the world to condemn the world, but in order that the world might be saved through him.

John 3:16-17

For by grace you have been saved through faith. And this is not your own doing; it is the gift of God, not a result of works, so that no one may boast.

Ephesians 2:8-9

If you confess with your mouth that Jesus is Lord and believe in your heart that God raised him from the dead, you will be saved. For with the heart one believes and is justified, and with the mouth one confesses and is saved.

Romans 10:9-10

Because our sin has separated us from God, we need a savior, one who would take our place in eternal death and give us eternal life. Jesus is that savior; the only one qualified to take our place.

And this is the testimony, that God gave us eternal life, and this life is in his Son. Whoever has the Son has life; whoever does not have the Son of God does not have life.

1 John 5:11-12

Receive Christ right now by praying a prayer such as this one. Speak the words from your heart, and God will hear and answer you.

Dear God, I see that my sins have separated me from You and I repent of sin. Thank You that you loved me so much that You sent Jesus to suffer and die on my behalf, so that I could receive eternal life. I believe Jesus died for me and rose again, and I receive Him as my Savior right now. Jesus, You are my Lord and I'll live for You from this day on. Thank You Father for saving me!

If you prayed that and meant it, be assured that God has done exactly what you asked. You are now His child. You have been born into His family. This verse now describes you, the new creation:

Therefore, if anyone is in Christ, he is a new creation. The old has passed away; behold, the new has come.
2 Corinthians 5:17

There are some additional steps you should take now that you are a follower of Jesus Christ. The most important step is to find a good local church. The pastor there will minister to you and help you grow in the things of God. Make sure your church believes and teaches the Bible and allows the Holy Spirit to work freely. Your pastor can help teach you about other steps to get started in the Christian life, such as studying the Word of God, being filled with the Holy Spirit, tithing, and serving in the local church.

Congratulations on making life's most important decision!

About the Author

Faith in God's Word, and constant reliance on the Holy Spirit have been the keys to success in the life and ministry of Rev. Joel Siegel. Raised and educated as a Jew, Joel Siegel, at age 18, had a life-transforming encounter with Christ that brought him true purpose and fulfillment.

Rev. Joel Siegel began preaching and teaching the Word of God soon after he was saved in 1986. He entered full-time ministry in 1990, serving for three years as the music director for the acclaimed gospel music group *Truth*. Truth's road schedule took Joel and his wife Amy worldwide to over 300 cities a year, ministering in churches and on college campuses.

From 1993 to 2000, Joel was the musical director for Rev. Kenneth E. Hagin's RHEMA Singers & Band. In addition to assisting Rev. Hagin in his crusade meetings, Joel produced eight music projects for the ministry, including his first solo release, *Trust & Obey*.

From 2000 to 2011, Joel and Amy (herself a skilled pastor and worship leader), served as the founding pastors of Good News Family Church in Orchard Park, NY. During this time, they were frequently asked to host shows for the TCT Christian Television Network. Joel regularly hosted their popular *Ask The Pastor* program.

Rev. Joel Siegel spends his time ministering to congregations in the U.S. and abroad, passionately endeavoring to fulfill his assignment to help lead this generation into the move of God that will usher in the return of Christ.

The Siegels make their home in Colorado. Joel oversees Faith Church Colorado in the town of Castle Rock, where Amy is lead pastor.

For music recordings, audio teaching series, books, and other resources, or to invite Rev. Joel Siegel to minister at a church or event, please visit www.joelsiegel.org.